EGYPT 2016 HUMAN RIGHTS REPORT

EXECUTIVE SUMMARY

According to its constitution, Egypt is a republic governed by an elected president and unicameral legislature. Domestic and international observers concluded the presidential election that took place in 2014 was administered professionally and in line with the country's laws, while also expressing serious concerns that government limitations on association, assembly, and expression constrained broad political participation. Domestic and international observers also concluded that government authorities professionally administered the parliamentary elections that took place October through December 2015 in accordance with the country's laws, while also expressing concern about restrictions on freedom of peaceful assembly, association, and expression and their negative effect on the political climate surrounding the elections.

Civilian authorities maintained effective control over the security forces.

The most significant human rights problems were excessive use of force by security forces, deficiencies in due process, and the suppression of civil liberties. Excessive use of force included unlawful killings and torture. Due process problems included the excessive use of preventative custody and pretrial detention, the use of military courts to try civilians, trials involving hundreds of defendants in which authorities did not present evidence on an individual basis, and arrests conducted without warrants or judicial orders. Civil liberties problems included societal and government restrictions on freedoms of expression and the media, as well as on the freedoms of assembly and association in statute and practice.

Other human rights problems included disappearances; harsh prison conditions; arbitrary arrests; a judiciary that in some cases appeared to arrive at outcomes not supported by publicly available evidence or that appeared to reflect political motivations; reports of political prisoners and detainees; restrictions on academic freedom; impunity for security forces; harassment of some civil society organizations; limits on religious freedom; official corruption; limits on civil society organizations; violence, harassment, and societal discrimination against women and girls, including female genital mutilation/cutting (FGM/C); child abuse; discrimination against persons with disabilities; trafficking in persons; societal discrimination against religious minorities; discrimination and arrests based on sexual orientation; discrimination against HIV-positive persons; and worker abuse, including child labor.

The government inconsistently punished or prosecuted officials who committed abuses, whether in the security services or elsewhere in government. In most cases the government did not comprehensively investigate human rights abuses, including most incidents of violence by security forces, contributing to an environment of impunity.

Attacks by terrorist organizations caused arbitrary and unlawful deprivation of life. Terrorist groups conducted deadly attacks on government, civilian, and security targets throughout the country, including schools, places of worship, and public transportation.

Section 1. Respect for the Integrity of the Person, Including Freedom from:

a. Arbitrary Deprivation of Life and other Unlawful or Politically Motivated Killings

There were numerous reports that the government or its agents committed arbitrary or unlawful killings while making arrests or holding persons in custody. There were reports that the government or its agents committed arbitrary or unlawful killings during disputes with civilians. There were a few reports of such killings while the government or its agents dispersed demonstrations. There were also reports of civilians killed during military operations in the Sinai. Impunity was a problem.

There were instances of persons tortured to death and other allegations of killings in prisons and detention centers. Amnesty International (AI) reported eight deaths due to torture as of March 29. The government charged, prosecuted, and convicted perpetrators in some cases. On February 3, authorities found the body of Italian graduate student Giulio Regeni with what forensics officials said were signs of torture, including cigarette burns, broken bones, and head injuries. Local and international human rights groups stated such signs of torture were consistent with forms of abuse committed by security services. Some human rights groups further alleged torture by security services was responsible for Regeni's death. An international news agency reported security services detained Regeni prior to his death, citing intelligence and police sources. The Interior Ministry denied such claims and any connection with Regeni's death. As of November an investigative team led by the Prosecutor General's Office had not released its conclusions.

On November 13, authorities arrested Magdy Maken, a fish cart vendor, following an altercation with a police officer. His family's lawyer claimed police officers subsequently beat him in the streets before taking him to a police station in the neighborhood of el-Ameriyah and that several hour later authorities took his corpse to a nearby hospital with marks of torture. Videos of Maken's body posted on social media showed a bleeding backside and bruises on his face. Authorities stated they arrested Maken for possession of the painkiller tramadol and claimed he later died of diabetes-related complications. Authorities investigated 10 police officers in connection with the case. At year's end police captain Karim Madgy and three other officers were detained pending investigations, and six others were released on bail pending further investigations.

There were reports of suspects killed in unclear circumstances during or after arrest. On July 24, police detained Mohamed Samir and later beat him to death, according to Samir's family members' comments to media. The Interior Ministry stated Samir escaped from police while being escorted to a police station and authorities later found him dead in the Nile River.

There were reports of police killing unarmed civilians during personal or business disputes, which local academics and human rights groups claimed were part of a culture of excessive violence within security services. On April 2, a court sentenced police officer Mostafa Abdel Haseeb to life imprisonment after Haseeb killed a rickshaw driver in February during a dispute over a fare. On April 19, a police officer shot and killed a tea seller in New Cairo and injured two others after a dispute over the price of a cup of tea. According to media reports, witnesses stated there was an altercation between a police officer and a tea seller after the officer refused to pay for a cup of tea, and the officer shot the seller and a bystander who tried to intervene, killing the seller and injuring the bystander. On November 16, authorities convicted the police officer of murder and sentenced him to life in prison.

There were continued reports of suspected terrorists and other suspected criminals killed during security raids conducted by police. The Interior Ministry claimed police officers fired at suspects only when suspects fired first. Rights groups claimed these shootings might have amounted to extrajudicial killings. In some of these cases, media reported that family members said there was evidence that police detained suspects before killing them. On February 7, police reportedly killed four alleged members of the terrorist group Ajnad Misr during a raid on a house near central Cairo. The Interior Ministry claimed those killed were suspects in the killing of two police officers, a soldier, and a civilian. On March 24, police killed four members of a criminal gang during an exchange of gunfire in New Cairo, according to an Interior Ministry statement. The ministry alleged the gang members were responsible for killing Regeni (see above) and claimed that police found Regeni's passport at the gang's apartment. Family members of those killed denied these allegations, Italian investigators highlighted inconsistencies in the ministry's account linking the gang to Regeni, and the public prosecutor initially denied such a link.

On October 4, the Interior Ministry stated that security forces had killed a senior leader of a Muslim Brotherhood faction, Mohamed Kamal, whom it described as responsible for the group's "armed wing," as well as his aide, Yasser Shehata, in an exchange of gunfire during a raid on an apartment in Cairo's southern Bassateen District. A lawyer representing the two men's families told media they both surrendered as soon as police arrived around 6 p.m. on October 3, and after police searched their apartments, police shot the men.

The government used force, and at times used excessive force, to disperse both peaceful and nonpeaceful demonstrations. According to local media reports, on February 26, security forces shot and killed two protesters, al-Sayed Abu al-Maaty and Mohamed al-Badawi, who the Ministry of Interior claimed were members of the Muslim Brotherhood. The Interior Ministry stated the two men were armed and initiated the attack on security forces, while the Muslim Brotherhood claimed police and "thugs" fired randomly at the protesters.

On February 14, the Court of Cassation ordered a retrial in the case of the Central Security Forces officer previously convicted of killing secular activist Shaimaa el-Sabbagh at a peaceful demonstration in January 2015. A Cairo criminal court previously sentenced the officer to 15 years in prison for manslaughter (see section 1.d.). The retrial began in October, and the next hearing was scheduled for February 19, 2017.

Although there were claims that demonstrators sometimes instigated violence, there were no reports of investigations of loss of life during these incidents.

Rights groups and international media reported the armed forces used indiscriminate force during military operations that targeted widespread terrorist activity in the northern Sinai Peninsula, resulting in killings of civilians and destruction of property, particularly along the border with Gaza, where there was extensive smuggling of weapons and other equipment to terrorist groups. The government did not report any civilian casualties during operations in the Sinai.

On October 25, Egyptian security forces killed 15-year-old Israeli Bedouin Nimer Abu Amer, who was accompanying relatives employed in maintenance work on the border fence between Israel and Egypt by a contractor for the Israeli Ministry of Defense. An Egyptian security official told press a border guard mistook the teenager for a migrant attempting to cross the border illegally.

A government investigation continued into the killing of 12 persons, including eight Mexican citizens, in September 2015, when air force units mistakenly attacked a tourist convoy near the Bahariya oasis in the western desert while in pursuit of an armed militant group. The government alleged the company entered an unauthorized area without proper permits, while the company claimed it had the correct permits and an official escort. On May 9, the quasi-governmental Egyptian Travel Agents Association, a union of local tourism chambers of commerce, told press that it had paid the families of three of the victims 2.21 million Egyptian pounds (LE) ($120,000) each in compensation after they agreed to drop legal proceedings against Egypt. Negotiations continued with the other five families who lost relatives in the attack, according to the association.

In 2014 a court sentenced one police officer to 10 years in prison for manslaughter and three other officers to one-year suspended prison sentences in the 2013 case in which police killed 37 Muslim Brotherhood detainees while transferring them to Abu Zaabal Prison near Cairo. In 2014 an appeals court vacated the sentences and returned the case to the public prosecution for reinvestigation. In August 2015 the appeals court reduced the officer's sentence from 10 to five years and upheld the one-year suspended prison sentences for the three other officers. A second appeal was pending at year's end.

At year's end the government had not held accountable any individual or governmental body for state violence after June 2013, including the deaths of hundreds of civilians during the August 2013 dispersals of the sit-ins at Rabaa al-Adawiya Square in Cairo and Nahda Square in Giza.

Terrorist groups, including Da'esh Sinai Province (formerly known as Ansar Bayt al-Maqdis) and Ajnad Misr, among others, conducted deadly attacks on government, civilian, and security targets throughout the country, including schools, places of worship, and public transportation. On May 8, terrorists killed eight police officers in an attack on an unmarked police microbus in Helwan. Both a Da'esh Egyptian affiliate and terrorist group Popular Resistance claimed responsibility for the attack. On November 15, the press reported that authorities had arrested more than 30 suspects following the attacks. Official investigations continued at year's end.

In February the president acknowledged that terrorism caused the October 2015 crash of Metrojet flight 9268, which killed all 224 individuals on board. Da'esh Sinai Province claimed responsibility for the attack; official investigations of the crash continued at year's end.

On December 11, a terrorist attack during Mass at the Boutrusiya church, adjacent to the Coptic Orthodox Cathedral, killed 27 and injured dozens more, most of whom were women and children. Authorities stated that a suicide bomber collaborated with the Muslim Brotherhood to carry out the attack, a claim Muslim Brotherhood spokesmen denied. Da'esh later claimed responsibility for the attack

There was no published official data on the number of victims of terrorist violence during the year. According to local media reports, terrorists killed hundreds of civilians throughout the country. In Sinai alone, as of the end of October, militant violence had killed at least 230 civilians and 299 security force members (police and military), according to publicly available information. During the same period in Sinai, the government killed 2,436 terrorists, according to official public statements.

b. Disappearance

Several international and local human rights groups, including the quasi-governmental National Council on Human Rights (NCHR), reported a spike in enforced disappearances, alleging authorities increasingly relied on this tactic to intimidate critics. According to a July AI report, authorities had forcibly disappeared at least several hundred individuals since the beginning of 2015. In all of the cases AI presented, authorities arrested those forcibly disappeared in a manner that did not comply with due process laws (see section 1.d.). In most of the cases AI documented, authorities detained individuals after forcing their way into homes and, in all such cases, without producing arrest or search warrants. Authorities then allegedly detained many in police stations or Central Security Forces' camps but did not include them in official registers. Authorities held detainees incommunicado and denied their requests to contact family members and lawyers. The length of disappearances documented by AI ranged from a few days to seven months. In most cases according to AI, the period of disappearance ended when authorities took the detainee before a prosecutor for questioning. Local rights groups provided various estimates of forced disappearances, with one reporting 630 cases between January and May 15. According to its July 3 report, the NCHR raised 266 cases of enforced disappearances with the Interior Ministry, which had responded with information on 238 of those cases as of March. According to the report, the Interior Ministry was unable to locate 44 of the individuals identified by the NCHR.

On January 12, authorities detained 14-year-old Aser Mohamed, taking him from his home without producing an arrest warrant, according to his family, as reported by AI. Mohamed's family searched for him for the next 34 days. On February 15, Mohamed's family learned of his whereabouts, when Mohamed telephoned on his way to a Central Security Forces camp on the outskirts of Cairo, as stated by AI. During his time of enforced disappearance, according to his family's account, as described by AI, authorities reportedly tortured Mohamed to "confess" to participating in a terrorist attack and other crimes. After appearing before a prosecutor on February 15, authorities charged Mohamed with belonging to a banned group. As of July Mohamed remained at the Central Security Forces camp, according to AI. Mohamed's trial began in August, and the next hearing was scheduled for February 15.

Many victims of forced disappearance were held at the National Security Sector Lazoughly Office, according to AI. There were also reports that military authorities continued to hold civilians in secret at al-Azouly Prison inside al-Galaa Military Camp in Ismailia. Authorities did not charge the detainees with crimes or refer them to prosecutors or courts and prevented access to their lawyers and families.

According to a July 28 report of the UN Human Rights Council's Working Group on Enforced or Involuntary Disappearances, 226 disappearance cases were under the working group's review, an increase of more than 80 percent from the previous year. The report noted the working group's "extreme concern" with what appeared to be an increasing pattern of disappearances, notably short-term disappearances. By year's end the working group had not received a response to its 2011 request to visit the country (see section 5).

In March, after several statements by human rights groups on the increase in forced disappearances, the Interior Ministry claimed there were no forced disappearances in the country and no detainees held incommunicado or beyond judicial oversight in contravention of Egyptian law.

c. Torture and Other Cruel, Inhuman, or Degrading Treatment or Punishment

The constitution states that no torture, intimidation, coercion, or physical or moral harm shall be inflicted upon a person whose movements are restricted or whom authorities have detained or arrested. The penal code forbids torture to induce a confession from a detained or arrested suspect but fails to account for mental or psychological abuse against persons whom authorities have not formally accused, or for abuse occurring for reasons other than securing a confession. The penal code also forbids all public officials or civil servants from "employing cruelty" or "causing bodily harm" under any circumstances. Local rights organizations documented hundreds of incidents of torture throughout the year, including deaths that resulted from torture (see section 1.a.). According to domestic and international human rights organizations, police and prison guards sometimes resorted to torture to extract information from detainees, including minors. Reported techniques included beatings with fists, whips, rifle butts, and other objects; prolonged suspension by the limbs from a ceiling or door; electric shocks; sexual assault; attacks by dogs; and forced standing for hours. Government officials denied the use of torture was systemic. Authorities stated they did not sanction these abuses and, in some cases, prosecuted individual police officers for violating the law (see section 1.a.).

In an article published online on September 2, Ibrahim Halawa, an Irish-Egyptian citizen who authorities arrested in 2013 and remained in detention without bail (see section 2.d.) while his trial continued, claimed authorities tortured him while in prison, mostly through beatings. Authorities charged Halawa, along with 493 codefendants, with participating in a violent protest and other counts. Halawa's family stated that Halawa took refuge in al-Fath mosque during a dispersal of a protest nearby. Halawa's next hearing was scheduled for January 17.

A local rights group reported that authorities redetained 14-year-old Akram al-Sawy, along with his father, whom authorities accused of belonging to the Muslim Brotherhood, in January 2015, after Sawy described torture and abuse that authorities inflicted on Sawy and other prisoners at a Central Security Forces camp in Banha. Authorities previously detained both Sawy and his father from September 2014 until January 2015.

On July 12, a Luxor criminal court convicted six police officers of manslaughter in connection with the November 2015 death of 47-year-old Talaat Shebeeb in a Luxor police station hours after police arrested him. The Forensic Medical

Authority's report determined that a severe beating had broken the vertebrae in his back and severed his spinal cord. Authorities sentenced First Lieutenant Hani Samir to seven years in prison and five lower-ranked officers to three years. Authorities acquitted three other police officers and four soldiers charged in connection with Shebeeb's death.

No information was available about the results of the public prosecutor's investigation into a 2014 case in which police at the Matariya police station reportedly tortured to death a man they detained after a neighborhood quarrel. On February 3, a local human rights organization reported that 14 deaths in custody as a result of torture had occurred over the previous two years at this police station.

The United Nations reported that during the year (as of December 20) it received one allegation of sexual exploitation and abuse against Egyptian peacekeepers for an incident occurring in 2015. The Egyptian government investigated the allegation, which involved a military officer deployed to the UN Multidimensional Integrated Stabilization Mission in the Central African Republic, and found it to be substantiated. The officer was sentenced to five years' imprisonment.

Prison and Detention Center Conditions

Conditions in the prisons and detention centers were harsh and potentially life threatening due to overcrowding, physical abuse, inadequate medical care, poor infrastructure, and poor ventilation.

Physical Conditions: According to domestic and international nongovernmental organization (NGO) observers, prison cells were overcrowded, and prisoners lacked adequate access to medical care, proper sanitation and ventilation, food, and potable water. Tuberculosis was widespread. Provisions for temperature control and lighting generally were inadequate. Reports that guards abused prisoners, including juveniles, in adult facilities were common. Prison conditions for women were marginally better than those for men. Media reported that some prisoners protested conditions by going on hunger strikes, including at Aqrab Prison in February and March.

According to the law, religious books are required to be available for prisoners, religious counsel (including confession if appropriate) should be provided to prisoners in keeping with their religion prior to execution, and prisoners should not be compelled to work during religious holidays.

The large number of arrests and the use of pretrial detention during the year exacerbated harsh conditions and overcrowding, contributing to the prevalence of death in prisons and detention centers. In July the NCHR reported that prison populations were at 150 percent of maximum capacity and police station detention centers were at 300 percent of maximum capacity. Health care in prisons was inadequate, leading to a large number of prisoner deaths due to possibly treatable natural causes. Human rights groups and families of some deceased prisoners claimed that prison authorities denied prisoners access to potentially life-saving medical care and, in some cases, denied requests to transfer the prisoners to the hospital, leading to deaths in prison.

On April 26, Mamdouh Shaldam died in Burj al-Arab Prison after prison authorities denied him access to medical care needed to treat his hepatitis C, according to Shaldam's family, as reported by media.

There were reports authorities sometimes held prisoners accused of crimes related to political or security issues separately from common criminals and subjected them to verbal or physical abuse and punitive solitary confinement. Human rights lawyer Malek Adly was held in solitary confinement for more than 100 days in connection with protests against the government's announcement of a maritime border demarcation agreement with Saudi Arabia in which the government determined that Tiran and Sanafir islands fell under Saudi sovereignty. Rights groups alleged that his treatment while in detention, including being kept in solitary confinement, was to punish him for his work as a human rights lawyer. On August 28, Adly was released from prison pending investigation.

Authorities did not always separate juveniles from adults and sometimes held pretrial detainees with convicted prisoners. Rights organizations continued to allege the illegal use of Central Security Forces camps as detention facilities. In 2014 a local rights group claimed that authorities held at least 600 children between the ages of 14 and 17 at a Central Security Forces camp in Banha.

The law authorized prison officials to use force against prisoners who resisted orders.

Administration: The penal code provides for reasonable access to prisoners. The NCHR considered itself an ombudsman on behalf of prisoners, but there was no official ombudsman. According to NGO observers and relatives, the government sometimes prevented visitors' access to detainees. Prisoners could request investigation of alleged inhuman conditions. NGO observers claimed, however, that prisoners sometimes were reluctant to do so due to fear of retribution from prison officials. The government investigated some, but not all, of these allegations. As required by law, the public prosecutor continued to inspect prisons and detention centers.

Independent Monitoring: The government did not permit visits by nongovernmental observers but did permit some visits by the quasi-governmental NCHR to prisons and detention centers. The NCHR visited four prisons, one of which it visited twice, between January and November, after receiving approval from the Ministry of Interior's Prisons Authority or prosecutor general. The law formally recognizes the NCHR's role in monitoring prisons, specifying that visits require notifying the prosecutor general in advance. Authorities did not permit other organizations to conduct prison visits.

d. Arbitrary Arrest or Detention

The constitution prohibits arbitrary arrest and detention, but reported incidences of such practices remained high.

Role of the Police and Security Apparatus

The primary security forces of the Interior Ministry are the Public Police and the Central Security Forces. The Public Police are responsible for law enforcement nationwide. The Central Security Forces provide security for infrastructure and key domestic and foreign officials, and are responsible for crowd control. The National Security Sector, which investigates counterterrorism and internal security threats, also reports to the minister of interior. The armed forces report to the minister of defense and are generally responsible for external defense, but they also have a mandate to "assist" police in protecting "vital public facilities," including roads, bridges, railroads, power stations, and universities. Military personnel have arrest authority during "periods of significant turmoil." The Border Guards Department is responsible for border control and includes members from the army and police. Single-mission law enforcement agencies, such as the Tourist and Antiquities Police and the Antinarcotics General Administration, also worked throughout the country.

Civilian authorities maintained effective control over security forces. Official impunity, however, was a problem. Police investigative skills remained poor. Police did not investigate reported police abuses sufficiently, according to local and international human rights groups. The government investigated and prosecuted some, but not all, reports of abuse, and some prosecutions resulted in acquittals due to insufficient or contradictory evidence. The government frequently called for investigations of abuses by security forces, although these investigations rarely resulted in judicial punishment.

On February 14, the Court of Cassation ordered a retrial in the case of a Central Security Forces officer previously convicted of killing secular activist Shaimaa el-Sabbagh at a peaceful demonstration in January 2015. A Cairo criminal court previously sentenced the officer to 15 years in prison for manslaughter. The retrial began in October, and the next hearing was scheduled for February 19.

A retrial in the case against former president Hosni Mubarak, former minister of interior Habib al-Adly, and six others for issuing an order to kill protesters during the 2011 revolution continued at year's end. The retrial began in November 2015, and the next hearing was scheduled for March 2, 2017. By year's end authorities had not found any entity or individual responsible for the deaths of protesters during the 2011 revolution.

Arrest Procedures and Treatment of Detainees

For persons other than those apprehended in the process of committing a crime, the government required a warrant issued either under the penal code or the code of military justice, both of which were in effect simultaneously; however, there were reports of arrests without such a warrant.

Ordinary criminal courts and misdemeanor courts hear cases brought by the prosecutor general. Arrests under the penal code occurred openly and with warrants issued by a public prosecutor or judge. There was a functioning bail system, although some defendants claimed judges imposed unreasonably high bail.

Criminal defendants have the right to counsel promptly after arrest, and usually, but not always, authorities allowed access to family members. The court is obliged to provide a lawyer to indigent defendants. Nevertheless, defendants often faced administrative, and in some cases political, obstacles and could not secure regular access to lawyers or family visits. A prosecutor may order four days of preventative detention for individuals suspected of committing misdemeanors and 15 days for individuals suspected of committing felonies. This period of preventative detention is subject to renewal by the prosecutor for up to 60 days, in cases of both misdemeanors and felonies. On the 61st day, the prosecutor must submit a case to a relevant judge who can release the accused person or renew the detention in increments of 15 days (but no longer than 45 days at a time). This detention can extend from the stage of initial investigation through all stages of criminal judicial proceedings. Except in cases involving the death penalty or life imprisonment, the combined periods of prosecutor and court-ordered detentions cannot exceed six months in cases of misdemeanors and 18 months in cases of felonies. After the detention reaches its legal limit without a conviction, the accused person must be released immediately. Legal experts offered conflicting interpretations of the law in cases in which charges carry the death penalty or life imprisonment, with some arguing there is no time limit to court-ordered renewals of detention in such cases.

Charges involving the death penalty or life imprisonment sometimes could apply to cases related to demonstrations, such as blocking roads or demonstrating outside government buildings; as a result some appellants charged with nonviolent crimes might be held indefinitely.

Arbitrary Arrest: The constitution prohibits arrest, search, or detention without a judicial order, except for those caught in the act of a crime. There were frequent reports of arbitrary arrest and detention. Local activists and rights groups stated that hundreds of arrests did not comply with due-process laws. For example, authorities did not charge the detainees with crimes or refer them to prosecutors and prevented access to their lawyers and families (see section 1.b.).

Pretrial Detention: The government did not provide figures on the total number of pretrial detainees. Rights groups and the quasi-governmental NCHR alleged continued excessive use of pretrial detention and preventative detention during trials for nonviolent crimes. Authorities sometimes held pretrial detainees with convicted prisoners. Large backlogs in the criminal courts contributed to protracted periods of pretrial detention. Estimates of the number of pretrial and preventive detainees were unreliable. According to a May 10 report by the Egyptian Initiative for Personal Rights, at least 1,464 persons in four governorates remained in detention without bail for more than two years without a conviction and at various stages in the legal process. According to a May 2015 report by the NCHR, citing Interior Ministry figures, at least seven thousand persons remained in detention without a conviction at various stages in the legal process on charges related to incidents after June 2013, including approximately 300 "activists." Most others were affiliated with the Muslim Brotherhood, according to the NCHR.

Authorities have held spouses Aya Hijazi and Mohamed Hassanein, the two founders of the NGO Belady Foundation, in detention without bail since 2014.

Among other counts, authorities charged the two with torturing children, sexual assault, forcing children to participate in illegal demonstrations, and operation of a criminal group for the purposes of trafficking. Local human rights groups described such charges as baseless and depicted the delays in the defendants' trial as spurious. While the first trial hearing was held in March 2015, authorities delayed proceedings on procedural grounds several times, and the defense could not begin to argue its case until the fourth session, on February 13, according to local human rights groups. The next hearing was scheduled for January 14, 2017.

Authorities have held photojournalist Mahmoud Abu Zeid (known as Shawkan) in detention without bail since 2013. Authorities arrested him while he was taking pictures during the security forces' dispersal of the Muslim Brotherhood sit-in at Rabaa al-Adawiya Square in Cairo. Authorities charged Shawkan and 737 other defendants with belonging to the Muslim Brotherhood, possessing firearms, and murder. The court issued a decision to continue his detention during trial, according to his lawyers. The trial began in December 2015, but no substantive hearings had taken place by year's end. The next hearing was scheduled for January 17, 2017.

On March 25, authorities released Mahmoud Mohamed Hussein on bail of LE 1,000 ($55) pending investigations, after spending more than two years in detention in Cairo's Tora Prison. Authorities arrested then 17-year-old Hussein on a microbus in January 2014. According to AI, National Security Sector officers used electric shocks to his hands, back, and testicles to elicit a videotaped confession to membership in a banned group, possessing Molotov cocktails and hand grenades, protesting without authorization, and receiving money to protest.

<u>Detainee's Ability to Challenge Lawfulness of Detention before a Court</u>: According to the constitution, detainees have the right to challenge the legality of their detention before a court, which must decide if the detention is lawful within one week or otherwise immediately release the detainee. In practice authorities deprived some individuals of this right, according to international and local human rights groups.

<u>Protracted Detention of Rejected Asylum Seekers or Stateless Persons</u>: Authorities detained and sometimes deported without providing access to asylum procedures persons who entered the country illegally or who were present in the country illegally. As of September authorities detained 2,845 non-Egyptian foreign nationals attempting to depart from the north coast in an irregular manner. The majority were Sudanese (959) and Somalis (811), followed by Eritreans (379),

Comorians (302), and Ethiopians (300). Approximately 52 percent of those detained were registered refugees or asylum seekers, whom authorities usually quickly released. Others remained in detention without access to asylum procedures or due process. Those who authorities released could obtain and renew Egyptian residency permits, if registered as persons of concern to the Office of the UN High Commissioner for Refugees (UNHCR).

Authorities arrested and detained children, including unaccompanied children, without adequate access to food, clothing, sanitation, and health care, according to a local advocacy organization.

Amnesty: The constitution gives the president the power to grant a pardon or reduce a sentence, after consulting with the cabinet. The president used this authority to pardon hundreds of prisoners--generally those who had served the majority of their sentences during the year, including secular activists, student protesters, Muslim Brotherhood members, and others. According to press reports, the president had pardoned more than one thousand prisoners as of September. On May 4, authorities convicted and sentenced Sana Seif, a secular activist arrested in 2014 for breaking the demonstrations law and pardoned in 2015, to six months in prison for insulting a member of the prosecution by not complying with a summons on suspicion of inciting protests. Seif was released from prison on November 15 after completing her six-month sentence.

e. Denial of Fair Public Trial

The constitution provides for the independence and immunity of judges. Courts generally acted independently, although individual courts sometimes appeared to lack impartiality and to arrive at politically motivated outcomes or without individual findings of guilt. The government generally respected court orders. Judicial and executive review is available to individuals sentenced to the death penalty.

Some trials involving hundreds of defendants, particularly in cases involving demonstrators sympathetic to former president Morsy and the Muslim Brotherhood in 2013 and 2014, continued.

Retrials in two cases based in Minya with hundreds of defendants continued at year's end. In January 2015 the Court of Cassation ordered a retrial in the case in which a Minya court issued a provisional sentence condemning 529 persons to death on charges of killing a police officer and attempting to kill two other police officers. Authorities scheduled the next hearing for January 4, 2017.

In February 2015 the Court of Cassation ordered a retrial in the second high-profile Minya trial, in which the Minya Criminal Court issued provisional death sentences in 2014 to 683 defendants, including Muslim Brotherhood Supreme Guide Mohamed Badie, on charges of attacking a police station and killing two police officers. On December 28, a judge ordered the release of 13 defendants pending trial. The retrial continued, and the next hearing was scheduled for January 23, 2017.

An NGO, the International Commission on Jurists, alleged that authorities subjected judges who spoke out against attacks on the rule of law and human rights violations to unfair disciplinary proceedings. On October 18, Reuters reported that authorities forcibly retired 32 of 75 judges who had signed a document in 2013 criticizing the ouster of then president Morsy.

The constitution states: "Civilians cannot stand trial before military courts except for crimes that represent a direct assault against military facilities, military barracks, or whatever falls under their authority; stipulated military or border zones; military equipment, vehicles, weapons, ammunition, documents, military secrets, public funds or military factories; crimes related to conscription; or crimes that represent a direct assault against its officers or personnel because of the performance of their duties."

Nevertheless, authorities used military courts to try civilians during the year. Public access to information about military trials was limited. Military trials were difficult to monitor because they were usually subjected to media restraint orders. Rights groups and lawyers stated defense attorneys in military trials had difficulty gaining access to their clients and to documentation related to the cases.

In April, one local rights group alleged that military courts had tried at least 7,420 civilians, including at least 86 children, since the issuance of a 2014 decree ordering the military to "assist" police in securing "vital public facilities."

On May 29, AI reported that a military court sentenced eight civilians to death on charges including belonging to a banned group, possession of firearms and explosives, and obtaining classified information without authorization. The court also sentenced 18 codefendants to prison. The defendants bore signs of torture; however, authorities ignored their request to the court to be referred for evaluation by the Forensic Medical Authority, according to the defendants' lawyers, as reported by AI.

On February 16, a military court sentenced 116 individuals to life in prison, including then three-year-old Ahmed Mansour Qorani Sharara, on charges of murder, attempted murder, possession of firearms and explosives, and six other counts, according to media reports. Of the 116, authorities sentenced 100 in their absence, including Sharara. Authorities later said Sharara's inclusion in the case was due to mistaken identity and the court should have sentenced a 16-year-old with a similar name instead.

Former president Morsy remained in detention as a defendant in five cases brought by the prosecutor general in civilian court, all of which were in trial proceedings at year's end. The charges included incitement to murder, murder, fraud, insulting the judiciary, and espionage. Some local and international rights groups questioned the impartiality of proceedings. There were reports authorities periodically denied some family visit requests for security reasons.

Trial Procedures

The law presumes defendants are innocent, and authorities usually inform them promptly and in detail of charges against them. Defendants have the right to be present at their trials. Attendance is mandatory for individuals charged with felonies and optional for those charged with misdemeanors. Civilian criminal and misdemeanor trials usually are public. Defendants have the right to consult an attorney, and the government is responsible for providing counsel if the defendant cannot afford a lawyer. Defendants have the right to free interpretation from the moment charged through all appeals. An interpreter is assigned by the court. The law allows defendants to question witnesses against them and to present witnesses and evidence on their own behalf, and it provides defendants and their attorneys the right to access government-held evidence. Defendants have adequate time and facilities to prepare a defense. The constitution provides for the right of an accused person to remain silent in his own trial. In civilian courts defendants have the right of appeal up to the Court of Cassation. In civilian courts the judge must seek the nonbinding review of the Grand Mufti on all death sentences, and the president must confirm all such sentences.

The law permits individual members of the public to file charges with the prosecutor general, who is charged with deciding whether the evidence justifies referring the charges for a trial. Observers reported, however, that, due to unclear evidentiary standards, the Prosecutor General's Office investigates and refers for trial the overwhelming majority of such cases, regardless of the strength of the evidence.

Military courts are not open to the public. Defendants in military courts nominally enjoyed the same due process rights, but the military judiciary has wide discretion to curtail these rights in the name of public security. Military courts, however, often tried defendants in a matter of hours, frequently in groups, and sometimes without access to an attorney, leading lawyers and NGOs to assert they did not meet basic standards of due process. Consequently, the quick rulings by military courts sometimes prevented defendants from exercising their rights. Defendants in military courts have the right to consult an attorney, but sometimes authorities denied them timely access to counsel. According to rights groups, authorities permitted defendants in military trials visits from their attorneys every six months, in contrast with the civilian court system, where authorities allowed defendants in detention attorney visits every 15 days.

The Military Judiciary Law governing the military court system grants defendants in the military court system the right to appeal up to the Supreme Military Court of Appeals. The president must certify sentences by military courts.

Political Prisoners and Detainees

There were reports of political prisoners and detainees, although verifiable estimates were not available. The government claimed there were no political prisoners and all persons in detention had been or were in the process of being, charged with a crime. Human rights groups and international observers maintained the government detained or imprisoned as many as several thousand persons solely or chiefly because of their political beliefs or opposition to the government. One local rights organization estimated there were 60,000 political prisoners. A local rights group considered any persons arrested under the 2013 demonstrations law to be political prisoners. In their view these persons were political prisoners or detainees because authorities held them based on laws that restricted the exercise of a human right, because charges were false or inflated motivated by the individual's political opinion or membership in a particular group, or because some individuals faced unduly harsh and disproportionate treatment due to their political opinions or membership in particular groups.

Civil Judicial Procedures and Remedies

Individuals had access to civil courts for lawsuits relating to human rights violations and filed such lawsuits during the year. Nonetheless, courts often dismissed cases or acquitted defendants for lack of evidence or conflicting witness testimonies. Individuals and organizations can appeal adverse domestic decisions to the African Commission on Human and Peoples' Rights.

Property Restitution

In response to a continuing terrorist insurgency in North Sinai, the government continued its efforts to establish a buffer zone in the region to interdict weapons smuggling and incursions to and from the Gaza Strip. According to government statements to the media, authorities demolished 3,272 residential, commercial, administrative, and community buildings between mid-2013 and August. Human rights groups alleged that the military had evicted without adequate notice thousands of persons as part of the demolitions. The government promised it would appropriately compensate all families whose homes it destroyed. Some persons complained they did not receive adequate or timely restitution. The government did not compensate residents for agricultural land.

f. Arbitrary or Unlawful Interference with Privacy, Family, Home, or Correspondence

The constitution provides for the privacy of the home, correspondence, telephone calls, and other means of communication. There were reports security agencies sometimes placed political activists, suspected subversives, journalists, foreigners, and writers under surveillance; monitored their private communications; screened their correspondence, including e-mail and social media accounts; examined their bank records; searched their persons and homes without judicial authorization; and confiscated personal property in an extrajudicial manner.

Section 2. Respect for Civil Liberties, Including:

a. Freedom of Speech and Press

The constitution provides for freedom of speech and of the press but includes a clause stating, "it may be subject to limited censorship in times of war or public mobilization."

Freedom of Speech and Expression: Citizens expressed their views on a wide range of political and social topics. The government investigated and prosecuted critics for alleged incitement of violence, insults to religion, insults to public figures and institutions such as the judiciary and the military, or violation of public morals. Individuals also faced societal and official harassment for speech viewed as sympathetic to the Muslim Brotherhood, such as using a hand gesture showing four fingers, a reference to the 2013 security operation to disperse the sit-in at Rabaa al-Adawiya Square.

The law provides a broad definition of terrorism, to include "any act harming national unity or social peace." The president stated in a September speech that lying was a form of terrorism. Human rights observers expressed concern that authorities could use the ambiguous definition to stifle nonviolent speech and nonviolent opposition activity.

On February 20, a Bulaq Abu el-Ela appellate misdemeanor court sentenced author Ahmed Naji to two years in prison on charges of violating public morals based on the publication of an excerpt of his novel, *The Use of Life*, which contained explicit descriptions of sexual acts and illegal drug use. Authorities had acquitted Naji of the same charges in January, but prosecutors appealed the decision. Numerous writers and intellectuals decried the verdict, describing it as part of a larger government campaign against free expression. On December 18, a court suspended the implementation of Naji's sentence pending the appeal of his sentence. Naji's next hearing was scheduled for January 1, 2017.

In May authorities arrested the five members of the satirical group Street Children after it released a video criticizing supporters of the president and the increasing number of arrests. Band members were reportedly under investigation on charges of attempting to topple the regime, publishing offensive videos, and inciting citizens against authorities. In May authorities released one band member on bail and released the remaining four members in September pending investigations.

Press and Media Freedoms: The constitution, penal code, and media and publications law govern media issues. The government regulated the licensing of newspapers and controlled the printing and distribution of a majority of newspapers, including private newspapers and those of opposition political parties. The law does not impose restrictions on newspaper ownership.

The more than 20 state-owned media outlets broadly supported official state policy. The term for the governmental Higher Press Council, which had the power to appoint and dismiss editorial leadership of state-owned print outlets, expired in January. The governmental Egyptian Radio and Television Union appointed the heads of state-owned radio and television channels. Both state-owned and private media (including television and online journalism) sometimes criticized the government, but dominant media narratives supported the president and his policy initiatives.

As of December the Committee to Protect Journalists reported there were 25 imprisoned journalists in the country. Authorities continued to keep journalist Ismail Alexandrani in detention without formal charges at year's end. Authorities detained him in November 2015 on arrival at Hurgada airport. On November 20, a court ordered his release, but authorities successfully appealed the release order. According to local rights groups, Alexandrani was under investigation for "reporting false news" and "joining a banned group." Alexandrani's reporting and scholarly work focused on the Sinai.

On May 1, authorities raided the press syndicate headquarters and arrested two journalists, Mahmoud el-Sakka and Amr Badr, according to members of the syndicate. Both journalists worked for an opposition news site, *Bawabet Yanayer*. The Interior Ministry claimed it had not raided the headquarters, and the journalists had willingly surrendered to authorities. Authorities referred el-Sakka and Badr to trial on charges of spreading false news and possession of firearms and Molotov cocktails. On August 27, a court ordered Badr's release on bail of LE 5,000 ($275) pending investigations. On September 29, a court ordered el-Sakka's release on bail of LE 5,000 ($275) pending investigations. The journalists' arrests followed arrests of dozens of others on April 25, in connection with protests against the government's announcement of a maritime border demarcation agreement with Saudi Arabia in which the government determined that Tiran and Sanafir islands fell under Saudi sovereignty. According to a local rights group, authorities released most of those detained that day after a short incarceration.

On November 19, a court sentenced Yehia Kalash, president of the press syndicate, and Gamal Abdel Reheem and Khaled el-Balshy, two syndicate board members, to two years in prison for harboring fugitives (el-Sakka and Badr) inside the syndicate's headquarters and spreading false news in connection with the May 1 raid on the syndicate headquarters. The three were sentenced in absentia; they appealed the verdict, and the hearing was scheduled for January 14, 2017.

On August 27, according to media reports, an administrative court referred Azza al-Henawy, an anchor for state-owned al-Qahera TV, to trial on charges including insulting the president. Al-Henawy had criticized the president and made allegations of corruption during a March television broadcast.

The Ministry of Foreign Affairs issued statements condemning articles critical of the country in international publications, sometimes citing the authors by name.

Violence and Harassment: According to media reports and local and international human rights groups, state and nonstate actors arrested and imprisoned, harassed, and intimidated journalists. Foreign correspondents reported cases where the government denied them entry, deported them, and delayed or denied issuance of media credentials; some claimed these actions were part of a government campaign to intimidate foreign media.

On May 23, authorities denied French news correspondent Remy Pigaglio entry into the country when he arrived at Cairo International Airport after returning from vacation in France. Pigaglio claimed officials at first prevented him from contacting the French ambassador in Egypt and, and after detaining him for more than 24 hours, deported him.

In June security officers took British-Lebanese journalist Lilian Daoud from her Cairo home by security officers immediately following the end of her employment contract with ONTV. Authorities briefly detained and then deported her, according to media reports. On her television show, *The Full Picture*, Daoud had hosted protesters and youth leaders as well as government officials. The program had expressed views critical of the government.

In September 2015 the Cairo Criminal Court began a trial of 48 defendants accused of being Muslim Brotherhood members and charged with participating in the 2014 protest in Ain Shams during which journalist Mayada Ashraf was shot and killed while covering the clashes between protesters and police. The next hearing was scheduled for February 13, 2017.

Censorship or Content Restrictions: Official censorship occurred. On February 3, art-house cinema Zawya stated that the country's Censorship Authority refused to authorize the screening of three short films as part of Zawya's Short Film Festival. Zawya's director speculated to media that in the case of two of the three films, authorities objected to the content of the films, which included sexual content and discussions of atheism.

In August government officials confiscated copies of an issue of privately owned *Sout Alomma* newspaper, which included an article about the health of the president's mother and articles critical of former president Hosni Mubarak.

Some activists and many journalists reported privately they self-censored criticism of the government or comments that could be perceived as sympathetic to the Muslim Brotherhood, due to the overall anti-Muslim Brotherhood and progovernment media environment. Publishers were also wary of publishing books that criticized religious institutions, such as al-Azhar, or challenged Islamic doctrine.

Libel/Slander Laws: Local and international rights groups reported several cases of authorities charging and convicting individuals with denigrating religion under the so-called blasphemy law, primarily targeting Christians but also Muslims.

On January 26, al-Khalifa Misdemeanor Court convicted writer Fatima Naoot in her absence and sentenced her to three years in prison and a fine of LE 20,000 ($1,100) for denigrating Islam by describing the Islamic ritual of sacrificing sheep during Eid al-Adha as a "massacre," in a 2014 Facebook post. On March 31, the Sayeda Zeinab Appellate Misdemeanor Court confirmed the sentence. After Naoot appealed the decision, on October 20, the same court ordered her release pending investigations. On November 24, an appeals court reduced her sentence to a six months suspended.

On February 25, Bani Mazar Juvenile Misdemeanor Court sentenced four Christian high school students to five years' imprisonment for denigrating Islam after the students appeared in video pretending to perform a Muslim prayer. The same court sentenced the students' teacher, Gad Youssef Younan, who reportedly filmed the video, to three years in prison for denigrating Islam in December 2015.

Authorities released Mohamed Hegazy, also known as Bishoy Armia Boulous, from prison in July after spending more than two years in detention based on accusations that he had denigrated Islam in a symposium in 2009. A court ordered his release in June; however, over a period of several weeks, prison authorities claimed to have lost the court order and moved him to another prison without informing his attorney, according to media reports. During this time Hegazy recorded a video from prison in which he stated that he was reverting to Islam from Christianity; authorities released him shortly thereafter. Boulous unsuccessfully sued the Ministry of Interior in 2009 to recognize his conversion from Islam to Christianity, testing the constitutional right of freedom of religion.

National Security: The law allows government censors to block the publication of information related to intelligence and national security. Judges may issue and have issued restraint orders to prevent media from covering court cases considered sensitive on national security grounds. Rights groups stated authorities sometimes misused the orders to shield government, police, or military officials from public scrutiny. For example, on April 30, a court issued such an order in the case of protesters arrested during demonstrations against the government's announcement of a maritime border demarcation agreement with Saudi Arabia in which the bilateral agreement determined that Tiran and Sanafir islands fall under Saudi sovereignty. Citing safety and security, the government and military restricted media access to many parts of North Sinai.

The law imposes a fine on any person who "intentionally publishes…or spreads false news" contradicting official Ministry of Defense statements. The fine is many times the average annual salary of most local journalists.

An amendment to the police authority law, approved by parliament on August 9, bars police from providing information related to their work to media without permission from the Interior Ministry. An international NGO argued the amendment illustrated the government's continuing effort to undermine transparency.

Internet Freedom

The government did not generally restrict or disrupt access to the internet or censor online content, albeit with some exceptions. The constitution protects the right to privacy, including on the internet. The constitution provides for the confidentiality and "inviolability" of postal, telegraphic, and electronic correspondence; telephone calls; and other means of communication. They may not be confiscated, revealed, or monitored except with a judicial order, only for a definite period, and only in cases defined by law. The constitution prohibits the government from "arbitrarily" interrupting, disconnecting, or depriving citizens seeking to use all forms of internet communications. Law enforcement agencies occasionally restricted or disrupted individuals' access to the internet, and the government monitored social media accounts and internet usage, relying on a law that only allows targeted interception of communications under judicial oversight for a limited period of time and does not permit indiscriminate mass surveillance. The public prosecutor occasionally prosecuted individuals accused of posting "insulting" material.

The counterterrorism law criminalizes the use of the internet to "promote ideas or beliefs that call for terrorist acts" or to "broadcast what is intended to mislead security authorities or influence the course of justice in relation to any terrorist crime." The law also authorizes the public prosecutor and investigators to monitor and record online communications between suspects in terrorism cases for a period of 30 days, renewable in 30-day increments. The law does not specify a maximum time period.

The government attempted to disrupt the communications of terrorist groups operating in northern Sinai by cutting telecommunication networks: mobile services, internet, and sometimes landlines. Cuts generally occurred from 6 a.m. to 6 p.m. Networks were again fully accessible at approximately 8 p.m. and sometimes later. This tactic disrupted operations of government facilities and banks. The law obliges internet service providers and mobile operators to allow government access to customer databases, which can allow security forces to obtain information about activities of specific customers, which could lead to lack of online anonymity. Individuals widely used social media sites, such as Twitter and Facebook, during demonstrations and included widespread criticism of the government and security forces.

In July, Internet Live Stats estimated internet penetration to be 33 percent. A local civil society organization estimated 57 percent of families had internet access at home and four million persons used Twitter. A digital consulting company stated 28 million persons used Facebook.

There were reports that authorities monitored social media and internet dating sites to identify and arrest lesbian, gay, bisexual, transgender, and intersex (LGBTI) individuals (see section 6, Acts of Violence, Discrimination, and Other Abuses Based on Sexual Orientation and Gender Identity).

On January 13, police arrested three administrators of Facebook pages that allegedly promoted antigovernment protests scheduled for the fifth anniversary of the January 25 Revolution, according to media reports. Two of the three were Muslim Brotherhood members, according to state-owned media.

In April international media reported that in December 2015 Facebook terminated its Free Basics Service, which provided mobile phone users with free access to a limited suite of internet services, because the company would not allow the government to circumvent the service's security to conduct surveillance. The government previously stated that it had only granted the mobile carrier Etisalat a temporary permit to offer the service for two months.

On December 19, Open Whisper Systems claimed that Egyptian authorities were blocking access to its encrypted messaging application Signal.

Academic Freedom and Cultural Events

There were reports of government restrictions on academic freedom. In October, Minister of Higher Education Ashraf al-Shihy published a statement requiring private universities to review all research papers and thesis dissertations to assure they do not include any "direct or indirect insult to societies or individuals belonging to any brotherly or friendly countries." According to media and local rights groups, a degree of self-censorship, similar to that reported by nonacademic commentators, allegedly existed when academics publicly commented on sensitive political and socioeconomic issues. In February media reported that in December 2015, Cairo University revoked permission for one of its professors, Kholoud Saber, to pursue her doctoral degree abroad. Saber told media the decision came from an office connected to the Interior Ministry. Separately, Cairo University President Gaber Nassar told media that security forces did not intervene in the university's academic affairs. Days after publication of the news reports, Cairo University reversed its decision to revoke Saber's permission to study abroad.

There was censorship of cultural events. The Ministry of Culture must approve all scripts and final productions of plays and films. The ministry censored foreign films to be shown in theaters but did not censor the same films sold as DVDs.

On January 20, authorities cancelled a scheduled concert by the band Elawela Balady, according to an announcement by the group, which is widely associated with the January 25 Revolution. A local human rights group described the move as an attempt by authorities to silence voices connected to the revolution.

Independent film center, Cimatheque, associated with Khaled Abdalla from the prominent revolutionary documentary *The Square* and the sister production company Zero Productions, remained closed since October 2015 and received regular visits from authorities. In February authorities allowed Townhouse Gallery of Contemporary Art, which was closed by authorities in December 2015, to reopen under what its director told press were new legal restrictions; he alleged that some restrictions amounted to state control of its work. Townhouse's affiliated Rawabet Theater, which was also raided in December 2015, also reopened. The Merit Publishing House, which authorities raided in December 2015, remained open. Authorities quickly released the Merit employee detained in December 2015.

b. Freedom of Peaceful Assembly and Association

Freedom of Assembly

The constitution provides for freedom of assembly "according to notification regulated by law." Authorities implemented a 2013 demonstrations law that includes an expansive list of prohibited activities and gives the minister of interior the authority to prohibit or curtail planned demonstrations. Domestic and international human rights organizations asserted the law was not in keeping with international standards regarding freedom of assembly. There were protests throughout the year that varied widely in size, and some occurred without government interference. In other cases the government rigorously enforced the law restricting demonstrations, even in cases of small groups of protesters demonstrating peacefully.

Research center Daftar Ahwal reported at least 37,059 cases of individuals being stopped, arrested, or charged under the protest law between November 2013 and September. Of these, authorities charged 15,491 individuals under the protest law resulting in 6,382 convictions and 5,083 acquittals.

In January security forces arrested more than 150 individuals in connection with protests on the fifth anniversary of the January 25 Revolution, according to media reports.

In February 2015 the Cairo Criminal Court sentenced prominent activist Alaa Abdel Fattah to five years in prison on charges of breaking the demonstrations law related to his participation in a protest in front of the Shura Council in 2013. The ruling was subject to appeal to the Court of Cassation, which at year's end had not ruled whether it would accept the appeal.

Authorities arrested at least 382 persons in the days leading to April 25 protests against the government's announcement of a maritime border demarcation agreement with Saudi Arabia that determined Tiran and Sanafir islands fall under Saudi sovereignty, according to an international rights organization. Authorities convicted many of these under the protest law; however, upon appeal authorities overturned many of the convictions or reduced sentences. For example, on May 24, a Dokki and Agouza court sentenced 111 individuals to five years' imprisonment in connection with the protests. The following day, the Dokki Misdemeanor Court cancelled the prison sentences but upheld fines of LE 100,000

($5,500) for 86 of the defendants and refused their request to pay the fines in installments.

Thousands of persons remained imprisoned whom authorities arrested during 2013 and 2014 due to their participation in demonstrations (some of which were peaceful); however, authorities released others who had completed their sentences. Authorities held such individuals under charges of attending an unauthorized protest, incitement to violence, or "blocking roads." Human rights groups claimed authorities inflated or used these charges solely to target individuals suspected of being members of groups in opposition to the government or those who sought to exercise the rights to free assembly or association.

Demonstrations on university campuses decreased throughout the country as compared with the previous academic year, but security forces continued to disperse them forcefully, according to a local rights group. In April student mobilization increased with students protesting the government's announcement of a maritime border demarcation agreement with Saudi Arabia that determined Tiran and Sanafir islands fall under Saudi sovereignty. According to the same local rights group, authorities arrested 84 students and expelled 47 students during the 2015-16 academic year.

Freedom of Association

The constitution and the 2013 constitutional declaration provide for freedom of association. The law governing associations, however, significantly restricts this right. The law on associations affects all nongovernmental civil society associations, the overwhelming majority of which were domestic welfare, educational, and environmental foundations. The Ministry of Social Solidarity applied the law in a highly restrictive manner on international and domestic organizations receiving international funding, denying government approval of programs that domestic and international organizations sought to implement or granting governmental approval after lengthy delays (which in some cases amounted to effective denials). Rights groups reported several incidents of security services ordering the cancellation of planned training programs or other events. Over the course of one week in May, the Ministry of Social Solidarity closed 75 NGOs in Beheira Governorate, according to a ministry statement. The ministry alleged all of the 75 had Muslim Brotherhood connections and claimed the governorate was "free" of any NGOs receiving foreign funding as a result of the closures.

The penal code criminalizes the request for or acceptance of foreign funds, materiel, weapons, ammunition, or "other things" from states or NGOs "with the intent to harm the national interest." Violators may be sentenced to life in prison, or the death penalty in the case of public officials and for crimes committed during times of war or with "terrorist purpose." The broad language raised concern among civil society that the article could be used to prosecute NGOs receiving or requesting international funding.

At year's end the conviction of 27 mostly foreign NGO workers sentenced in 2013 for operating unlicensed organizations and receiving foreign funding without government permission stood. Appeals for some defendants were pending at year's end; defendants had not yet filed appeals in the remainder of cases.

The Muslim Brotherhood, the Muslim Brotherhood-affiliated Freedom and Justice Party, and its NGO remained illegal, and the Muslim Brotherhood was a legally designated terrorist organization.

Authorities reopened investigations of local NGOs that received foreign funding under a case originally brought in 2011, and on December 7, human rights attorney Azza Soliman was arrested in connection with the case. She was subsequently released on bail pending investigations. On December 14, a Cairo criminal court ordered asset freezes against Soliman and the law firm she headed, Lawyers for Justice and Peace. Separately in the case, on September 17, a Cairo criminal court ordered asset freezes against five individuals--including Hossam Bahgat, founder of the Egyptian Initiative for Personal Rights; Gamal Eid, executive director of the Arabic Network for Human Rights Information; and Bahey el-Din Hassan, director of the Cairo Institute for Human Rights Studies (CIHRS)--and three organizations, including CIHRS, the Hisham Mubarak Law Center, and Egyptian Center for the Right to Education. The court denied a request to freeze the assets of six others including family members of those whose accounts were ordered frozen and support staff of the NGOs. On June 15, a Cairo criminal court ordered asset freezes against the Andalus Institute for Tolerance and Anti-Violence Studies and its director, Ahmed Samieh. Freeze orders are subject to appeal after three months. Asset freeze cases were also pending against women's rights organization Nazra for Feminist Studies and its executive director Mozn Hassan at year's end. The next hearing was scheduled for January 11, 2017.

In February el-Nadeem Center for the Rehabilitation of Victims of Violence (also registered under the name el-Nadeem for Psychological Rehabilitation), which documents torture and other forms of abuse and provides counseling for torture and rape victims, received administrative closure orders from three governmental bodies. The organization asserted the letters were politically motivated, targeting el-Nadeem because of its work on torture, deaths in detention, and impunity for these crimes. At year's end authorities had neither rescinded nor enforced the orders, and the organization continued to operate but had suspended its clinical activities

On February 29, a misdemeanor court sentenced Amr Ali, coordinator of the April 6 Youth Movement, a political advocacy group, to three years' imprisonment for inciting protests and attempting to topple the government. On July 30, an appeals court reduced his sentence to two years.

In March student union leaders called for a general assembly meeting to discuss the future of the Egyptian Student Union--the largest countrywide student union-- after the December 2015 decision by the Ministry of Higher Education to nullify the results of the union's November 2015 elections. As of December no such assembly had taken place.

c. Freedom of Religion

See the Department of State's *International Religious Freedom Report* at www.state.gov/religiousfreedomreport/.

d. Freedom of Movement, Internally Displaced Persons, Protection of Refugees, and Stateless Persons

The law provides for freedom of movement within the country, foreign travel, emigration, and repatriation, and the government generally respected these rights, albeit with some exceptions, including the handling of potential refugees and asylum seekers. The authorities maintained a "no-fly" list that prevented some defendants in court cases from fleeing the country.

Abuse of Migrants, Refugees, and Stateless Persons: Media, NGOs, and UNHCR staff reported multiple cases of attacks against refugees, particularly women and children. According to UNHCR, refugees reported harassment, sexual harassment, and discrimination. Refugee women and girls, particularly sub-Saharan Africans, faced significant societal, sexual, and gender-based violence.

According to a local civil society organization, police security sweeps increased in neighborhoods known to house Syrian, Sudanese, and other African refugees, as well as migrants, resulting in increased detentions. Detainees reported authorities subjected them to racist verbal abuse, beatings, and torture during detention.

While reports of abuse by Sinai-based facilitators and captors of illegal migrants continued to decline, a shift in human trafficking activities to mainland Egypt has accompanied this decline as a result of the security situation in Sinai and Libya.

Although the government did not cooperate consistently with UNHCR and humanitarian organizations in providing protection and assistance to asylum seekers and other persons of concern, it allowed UNHCR access to registered refugees in detention.

In-country Movement: Citizens and foreigners may not travel in areas of the country designated as military zones. The government sought to prevent private individuals, journalists, and civil society activists from entering the Sinai Peninsula, stating it was to protect their safety; however, some persons avoiding government detection did enter the Sinai, particularly irregular migrants attempting to reach the Israeli border and the western border zone.

Foreign Travel: The constitution states, "No citizen may be prevented from leaving the State territory."

Men who have not completed compulsory military service, however, may not travel abroad or emigrate. National identification cards indicated completion of military service. Married Bahais and their children faced difficulties obtaining national identification cards because the government did not recognize Bahai marriages as legitimate. Some Bahai men of draft age were unable to establish they either had fulfilled or were exempt from military service and, therefore, were unable to obtain passports. Police officials reportedly forced unmarried young women, sometimes including those in their 30s, to present their father's written permission to obtain a passport and to travel abroad, although the law does not require such permission.

Authorities required citizens between the ages of 18 and 45 to obtain permission from the Interior Ministry to travel to 16 countries: Guinea, Indonesia, Israel, Jordan, Malaysia, South Africa, South Korea, Thailand, Yemen, Iraq, Lebanon, Libya, Qatar, Sudan, Syria, and Turkey. Enforcement of these regulations was sporadic. The government stated it intended these regulations to make it more difficult for citizens to join terrorist groups and to stop flight of criminals. These regulations also affected the ability of other individuals to travel outside the country.

The government increasingly imposed travel bans on human rights defenders and political activists. In March, *Mada Masr* reported there had been 554 cases of politically motivated banned entry and exit imposed by authorities in airports since 2011. In February local and human rights groups said that authorities intended to intimidate and silence human rights defenders. Several local and international human rights organizations reported a string of exit bans issued against human rights defenders and human rights activists.

Individuals connected with NGOs facing investigation as part of the reopened NGO foreign funding case faced travel bans. On June 27, authorities prevented women's rights activist Mozn Hassan from departing the country and informed her that the prosecutor general had issued an order banning her from travel at the request of one of the case's investigative judges. On July 15, authorities prevented human rights lawyer and member of the NCHR, Nasser Amin, from departing the country and told him that authorities had subjected him to a travel ban. According to statements by Amin's lawyer, the travel ban was part of the reopened NGO foreign-funding case.

In January 2015 authorities prevented democracy activist Esraa Abdel Fattah from departing the country and informed her that authorities had issued a travel ban in her name. She filed a lawsuit to challenge the ban, but the court dismissed the suit. Separately, in 2015 authorities confiscated the passport of human rights defender Mohamed Lotfy and prevented him from traveling to Berlin to deliver a statement before the German parliament on the eve of President Sisi's state visit to Germany in June 2015. Abdel Fattah and Lotfy continued to be unable to depart the country.

Exile: There was no government-imposed exile, and the constitution prohibits the government from expelling citizens or banning citizens from returning to the country. Some Mubarak- and Morsy-era politicians lived outside the country by choice and alleged they faced government threats of prosecution.

Protection of Refugees

Access to Asylum: The constitution provides for the protection of political refugees, but the laws do not provide for granting asylum or refugee status, and the government has not established a comprehensive legal regime for providing protection to refugees. The government granted UNHCR authority to make refugee status determinations. UNHCR does not register Libyan citizens, nor does it register or provide any assistance to Palestinian refugees in the country.

According to UNHCR, as of September there were approximately 192,000 registered refugees and asylum seekers in the country, coming mainly from Syria, Sudan, South Sudan, Ethiopia, Eritrea, and Iraq. The number of Syrian nationals newly registered as refugees increased since 2015. Observers attributed the increase to a new level of socioeconomic desperation among Syrians who had prolonged their stay in Egypt while depleting their assets, as well as an increase in new arrivals by way of Sudan, which remained the only country to which Syrians could travel without visas. As of August UNHCR reported 114,911 registered Syrian refugees in the country. The number of African refugees significantly increased during the year according to UNHCR, particularly among Ethiopian, Eritrean, and South Sudanese populations.

In 2012 and 2013 under the Morsy administration, the government accorded Syrians visa-free entry. Starting in mid-2013, the government applied a system of visa and security clearance requirements for Syrian nationals and Palestinian refugees from Syria, thus assuring no direct entries from Syria since Egypt lacked consular services there. UNHCR reported cases of prolonged separation of Syrian families in Egypt and family members in Syria, Libya, or the Gulf countries. The government rarely granted family reunification visas.

Since the regulations took effect in 2013, UNHCR stated authorities detained and deported dozens of Syrians who arrived in the country without a visa or with forged documents, usually to the transit countries from which they arrived, or to Turkey or Lebanon. According to UNHCR, the number of Syrians using forged documents to travel to the country increased during the year. Stricter visa restrictions imposed by Jordan and Turkey also resulted in the return of some Syrians to Egypt, where they remained in prolonged detention.

Reports of irregular movements of individuals, including asylum seekers, and of detention of foreign nationals attempting to depart the country irregularly remained numerous, after a dramatic increase in 2013. Syrians represented the largest portion of this group, which also included Sudanese, South Sudanese, Eritreans, Somalis, Ethiopians, and other Africans. UNHCR observed increased African irregular departures from the country, particularly Sudanese, Eritrean, and Ethiopian nationals. Irregular migrants continued to travel steadily through the land route from Sudan (Wedi Halfa/Abu Simbel). There were 4,913 reported deaths of irregular migrants in the Mediterranean during the year, an increase from 3,600 reported for 2015.

UNHCR access to detained registered refugees and asylum seekers was unscheduled and intermittent. According to UNHCR, authorities allowed access but only by request. Local rights groups faced continued resistance from the government when trying to interview detainees at Qanater men's and women's prisons outside Cairo, which housed the majority of detained refugees and asylum seekers. Authorities denied UNHCR access to unregistered asylum seekers at all prison and detention facilities, and UNHCR officials faced difficulties accessing prisoners to determine their status. The government subjected detained migrants, many of whom were Ethiopian, Eritrean, Sudanese, and Somali (and may have had a basis for asylum claims), to prolonged administrative detention for unauthorized entry or residence. Detained migrants--as unregistered asylum seekers--did not have access to UNHCR. Authorities often held them in jails, military camps, and regular prisons with convicted criminals.

Approximately three thousand Palestinian refugees from Syria were also present in the country, representing a significant decrease from 2015, which rights groups believed was a result of able-bodied men and teenage boys departing by sea to Europe as irregular migrants. The majority reportedly lived in Cairo. The Palestinian Authority mission in the country provided limited assistance to this population, who were not able to access UNHCR assistance provided to Syrians due to governmental restrictions. Despite UNHCR's mandate for Palestinians outside of the fields of operations of the UN Relief and Works Agency, the government denied UNHCR permission to provide services, reportedly in part due to a belief that allowing UNHCR registration would negate Palestinian refugees' right of return. Similar to 2014 authorities detained a few Palestinian refugees from Syria but promptly released them. The International Committee of the Red Cross (ICRC) mission in Cairo provided some humanitarian assistance to Palestinian refugees from Syria.

Refoulement: According to human rights advocates, migrants detained while attempting to enter the country irregularly were typically given two options: return to their country of origin or indefinite administrative detention. Because the government denied UNHCR access to unregistered detained migrants and asylum seekers, the number of potential asylum seekers returned to their countries was unknown. Authorities frequently encouraged those detained to choose to return to their countries of origin to avoid continued detention, even in cases where the individuals expressed a fear of return. Authorities also deported children to their countries of origin without their parents or an adult caregiver. In 2014 authorities deported children recognized as refugees by UNHCR to their country of origin without their mother or an adult caregiver. In September members of the humanitarian assistance community noted that the government did not deport every irregular migrant caught either crossing the country or trying to depart by sea but that this inconsistent approach was largely due to the government's severe budgetary constraints.

UNHCR stated the Syrian embassy implemented a restrictive policy regarding the renewal of expired passports of Syrian nationals in detention, regardless of the grounds for arrest. In such cases the Syrian embassy issued a travel document valid only for return to Syria; therefore, the absence of a valid national passport for Syrian refugees in detention resulted in either prolonged detention or forced repatriation. According to UNHCR reports, the Syrian embassy renewed passports on an individual basis in a few cases for released detainees. Syrian authorities generally refused to renew passports for persons who had registered with UNHCR.

Fewer Palestinian refugees from Syria entered the country in an illegal manner with the intention to travel to Europe. In a number of cases, in the absence of valid travel documents or inability to confirm their identities, they faced either detention or deportation.

Employment: There is no law granting refugees the right to work. Those seeking unauthorized employment were challenged by lack of jobs and societal discrimination, particularly against sub-Saharan Africans. Refugees who found work took low-paying jobs in the informal market, such as domestic servants, and were vulnerable to financial and sexual exploitation by employers.

Access to Basic Services: Refugees, in particular non-Arabic-speaking refugees from sub-Saharan Africa, continued to face limited access to housing, public education, public health services, and other social services. The Interior Ministry restricted some international organizations seeking to assist migrants and refugees in the Sinai but provided the International Organization for Migration (IOM) access to some detention centers. UNHCR provided refugees with modest support for education and health care, as well as small monthly financial assistance grants for particularly vulnerable refugees. IOM provided additional assistance to particularly vulnerable migrants and individual asylum cases either rejected or being processed by UNHCR.

Some public schools enrolled Syrian refugee children, but universal access for refugee education was nonexistent largely due to concerns about overcrowded public schools and a lack of resources. Instead, refugee children mainly attended refugee-run schools, private schools, or were home schooled. The law requires government hospitals to provide free emergency medical care to refugees, but many of the hospitals did not have adequate resources to do so. In some cases hospitals insisted that refugees provide payment in advance of receiving services or refused to provide services to refugees. In response to the influx of Syrians, the government allowed Syrian refugees and asylum seekers access to public education and health services; however, due to lack of availability, the low quality of Egyptian public education, and cases of severe harassment of Syrian children, many Syrian children remained outside the formal education system.

Stateless Persons

Most of the 22 stateless persons known to UNHCR were Armenians displaced for more than 50 years. According to a local civil society organization, the number of stateless persons in the country was likely higher than the number recorded by UNHCR. The government and UNHCR lacked a mechanism for identifying stateless persons, including those of disputed Sudanese/South Sudanese nationality and those of disputed Ethiopian/Eritrean nationality. An unknown number of the approximately 50,000 to 100,000 Palestinian refugees were stateless.

Section 3. Freedom to Participate in the Political Process

The constitution provides citizens the ability to choose their government through the right to vote in free and fair periodic elections held by secret ballot and based on universal suffrage. Constraints on freedom of expression, association, and assembly, however, limited citizens' ability to do so.

Elections and Political Participation

<u>Recent Elections</u>: The country held parliamentary elections in several rounds October through December 2015. Domestic and international observers concluded that authorities administered parliamentary elections professionally and in accordance with the laws. Observers expressed concern about restrictions on freedoms of peaceful assembly, association, and expression and their negative effect on the political climate surrounding elections.

Domestic and international observers concluded authorities administered the 2014 presidential election professionally and in line with the law, but they expressed serious concerns regarding constraints on the freedoms of expression and association and limits on freedom of the press leading up to the election, which "prevented free political participation and severely compromised the broader electoral environment."

<u>Political Parties and Political Participation</u>: The constitution grants citizens the ability to form, register, and operate political parties. The law requires new parties to have a minimum of five thousand members from at least 10 governorates. The constitution also states, "no political activity may be practiced and no political parties may be formed on the basis of religion or discrimination based on gender, origin, or sectarian basis or geographic location. No activity that is hostile to democratic principles, secretive, or of military or quasi-military nature may be practiced. Political parties may not be dissolved except by virtue of a court judgment."

The Freedom and Justice Party, the political wing of the Muslim Brotherhood, remained banned. Authorities did not ban other Islamist parties, including the Strong Egypt Party and the Building and Development Party, although those parties boycotted the 2015 parliamentary elections, citing a "negative political environment." The Islamist al-Noor Party participated, winning 11 seats. In September, citing lack of jurisdiction, a court dismissed a lawsuit filed by a private individual demanding the dissolution of the al-Noor Party, among other parties alleged to have formed on a religious basis.

<u>Participation of Women and Minorities</u>: No laws limit the participation of women and members of minorities in the political process, and women and minorities participated. Social and cultural barriers, however, continued to limit women's political participation and leadership in most political parties and some government institutions. Voters elected a record number of 75 women, 36 Christians, and nine persons with disabilities to parliament during the 2015 elections, a substantial increase compared with the 2012 parliament, which included 11 women, 13 Christians, and no persons with disabilities. The House of Representatives law outlines the criteria for the electoral lists, which provides that the House of Representatives must include at least 56 women, 24 Christians, and nine persons with disabilities. In December 2015 the president appointed 28 additional members of parliament, including 14 women and two Christians. The House of Representatives law grants the president the authority to appoint House of Representatives members, not to surpass 5 percent of the total number of elected

members. If the president opts to use this authority, half of his appointments must be women, according to the law. Parliament included 89 women and 38 Christians.

Women led four cabinet ministries; not all cabinet members hold portfolios. No women or members of religious minorities were among the appointed governors of the 27 governorates. No women were on the Supreme Constitutional Court. Legal experts said there were approximately 66 female judges serving in family, criminal, economic, appeals, and misdemeanor courts; that total was less than 1 percent of judges. Several senior judges were Christian.

Section 4. Corruption and Lack of Transparency in Government

The law provides criminal penalties for official corruption, but the government did not consistently enforce the law. There were allegations members of the government, as well as the previous Mubarak and Morsy governments, engaged in corrupt practices with impunity. Court cases still pending at year's end were inconclusive regarding the accusations of impunity. The existing government pursued corruption cases against senior officials.

Corruption: The Central Agency for Auditing and Accounting (CAA) was the government's anticorruption body and submitted reports to the president and the prime minister that were not available to the public. The auditing and accounting agency stationed monitors at state-owned companies to report corrupt practices. The Administrative Control Authority, another independent body, had jurisdiction over state administrative bodies, state-owned enterprises, public associations and institutions, private companies undertaking public work, and organizations to which the state contributes in any form.

On March 28, the president dismissed the head of the CAA, Hehsam Geneina. In December 2015 Geneina publicly claimed that corruption in public and government circles led to the squandering and misappropriation of more than LE 600 billion ($33 million). In January a government fact-finding committee alleged that Geneina deliberately exaggerated figures about corruption for political purposes. Geneina told media that the allegations against him were politically motivated. On July 28, a Cairo court convicted Geneina of spreading false information, sentencing him to a one-year suspended prison term and a fine of LE 20,000 ($1,100). A court rejected Geneina's appeal on December 22 but suspended the implementation of his sentence for three years.

On January 9, the Court of Cassation rejected an appeal of a May 2015 Cairo criminal court conviction of former president Hosni Mubarak and his sons, Alaa Mubarak and Gamal Mubarak, on corruption charges, sentencing all three to three years' imprisonment. They were also fined collectively LE 21.2 million ($1.17 million) and ordered to repay LE 125 million ($6.9 million) in stolen funds. In October 2015 the court ordered the release of Alaa Mubarak and Gamal Mubarak from prison upon completion of their sentences. No further appeals are possible.

On March 12, the government announced it had reached a reconciliation agreement with businessman Hussein Salem. Salem had lived in Spain since 2011, following sentencing in his absence to 15 years in prison on corruption charges related to the sale of natural gas and 10 years in prison on corruption charges related to the sale of electricity. According to Salem's lawyer's comments to media, the agreement included the transfer of 78 percent of the assets held by Salem, his children, and his grandchildren to the government.

On April 11, a Cairo court sentenced former agriculture minister Salah Eddin Helal to 10 years in prison and a fine of LE one million ($55,100). The court convicted Salah and other ministry officials of accepting bribes to help businessmen illegally acquire state land. Salah appealed the decision, and court proceedings continued at year's end.

Financial Disclosure: There are no financial disclosure laws for public officials. A 2013 conflict-of-interest law forbids government officials from maintaining any pecuniary interest in matters over which they exercise authority.

Public Access to Information: There is no legal framework stipulating how citizens can access government information. The government generally was not responsive to requests for documents regarding government activities and did not provide reasons for its lack of responsiveness.

Section 5. Governmental Attitude Regarding International and Nongovernmental Investigation of Alleged Violations of Human Rights

The government continued to exhibit an uncooperative and suspicious approach to international and local human rights organizations. Government officials publicly asserted they shared the civil society organizations' goals, but they rarely cooperated with or responded to the organizations' inquiries. Domestic civil society organizations criticized the government's consultations with civil society as insufficient. Provisions in the NGO law and penal code for penalties of up to life imprisonment for requesting or accepting foreign funding to undermine state security continued to have a chilling effect on NGO operations (see section 2.b.).

Extended delays in gaining government approvals and an unclear legal environment continued to limit the ability of domestic and international NGOs to operate. State-owned and independent media frequently depicted NGOs, particularly international NGOs and domestic NGOs that received funding from international sources, as undertaking subversive activities. Some NGOs reported receiving visits or calls, to staff both at work and at home, from security service officers and tax officials monitoring their activities, as well as societal harassment.

Human rights defenders and political activists were also subjected to governmental and societal harassment and intimidation, for example, through travel bans (see section 2.d.). Print and television media published articles that included the names, photographs, business addresses, and alleged meetings held by activists, including meetings held with foreign diplomatic representatives.

Well-established, independent domestic human rights NGOs operated throughout the country. Internet activists and bloggers continued to play a significant role in publicizing information about human rights abuses. Authorities generally allowed civil society organizations not registered as NGOs to operate, but such organizations sometimes reported harassment, along with threats of government interference, investigation, asset freezes, or closure.

The government reopened investigations into the receipt of foreign funding by several human rights organizations (see section 1.b.).

Major international human rights organizations, such as Human Rights Watch (HRW) and AI, did not have offices in the country after closing them in 2014 due to "concerns about the deteriorating security and political environment in the country."

<u>The United Nations or Other International Bodies</u>: The government did not respond to the visit requests from eight UN special rapporteurs charged with investigation or monitoring of alleged human rights abuses, including the special rapporteurs for the independence of judges and lawyers; human rights defenders; freedom of religion; torture; arbitrary detention; extrajudicial, summary, or arbitrary execution; human rights and counterterrorism; and the freedom of association and assembly; as well as the UN Human Rights Council Working Group on Enforced or Involuntary Disappearances. The oldest pending request

was from the special rapporteur on torture in 1996. The most recent pending request was from the special rapporteur on the independence of judges and lawyers in 2014. The government had agreed to but not yet scheduled dates for the visits of four special rapporteurs, including those responsible for the sale of children, child prostitution, and child pornography; violence against women; promotion of truth, justice, reparation, and provision for their nonrecurrence; and foreign debt. All four requests had been outstanding for more than two years. Authorities did not allow the ICRC access to prisoners and detainees. The Interior Ministry provided some international organizations informal access to some detention centers where authorities detained asylum seekers, refugees, and migrants to provide humanitarian assistance (see section 2.d.).

Government Human Rights Bodies: The NCHR monitored government abuses of human rights and submitted citizen complaints to the government. A number of well-known human rights activists served on the organization's board, although some observers alleged the board's effectiveness was sometimes limited because it lacked sufficient resources and the government rarely acted on its findings. The council at times challenged and criticized government policies and practices, calling for steps to improve its human rights record. For example, the NCHR called for improved prison conditions and for repeal of the protest law.

Section 6. Discrimination, Societal Abuses, and Trafficking in Persons

Women

Rape and Domestic Violence: The law prohibits rape, although the legal definition of rape covers only forced penetration of the female sexual organ by the male sexual organ, prescribing criminal penalties of 15 to 25 years' imprisonment or life imprisonment for cases of rape involving armed abduction. Spousal rape is not illegal. The government did not effectively enforce the law. Civil society organizations reported police pressure not to pursue charges and fear of societal reprisal actively discouraged women from going to police stations to report crimes, resulting in a very small number of cases being investigated or effectively prosecuted. NGOs estimated the prevalence of rape was several times higher than the rate reported by the government.

Domestic violence continued to be a significant problem. According to the Egypt Economic Cost of Gender-Based Violence Survey (ECGBVS), published by the Central Agency for Public Mobilization and Statistics (CAPMAS), UN Fund Population (UNFPA), and National Council for Women (NCW), approximately

5.6 million women were exposed to violence perpetrated by a husband or fiance annually. The law does not prohibit domestic violence or spousal abuse, but authorities may apply provisions relating to assault with accompanying penalties. The law requires that an assault victim produce multiple eyewitnesses, a difficult condition for domestic abuse victims, making prosecutions extremely rare. NGOs reported police often treated domestic violence as a social rather than criminal matter.

Several NGOs offered counseling, legal aid, and other services to women who were victims of rape and domestic violence but operated under strained resources. The Ministry of Social Solidarity supported nine women's shelters. The Interior Ministry includes a unit responsible for combating sexual and gender-based violence. The NCW, a quasi-governmental body, was responsible for coordinating government and civil society efforts to empower women. In April 2015 the NCW launched a five-year National Strategy to Combat Violence Against Women with four strategic objectives: prevention, protection, intervention, and prosecution. As part of the strategy's implementation during the year, several ministries, in cooperation with UNFPA, developed a medical protocol for assisting survivors of violence and trained doctors in 172 hospitals as of May regarding how to implement the protocol. Additionally, authorities created a new forensic unit for violence against women and children. On June 26, the Ministry of Justice announced it had merged two assistant minister portfolios, creating an assistant minister of justice for human rights and the rights of the woman and child. The government assigned a female judge, who previously held the position of assistant minister of justice for the rights of the woman and child, as assistant minister of the combined portfolios.

Female Genital Mutilation/Cutting (FGM/C): FGM/C is illegal, but it remained a serious problem. According to the 2015 Egypt Health Issues Survey (EHIS), published during the year by the Ministry of Health and Population, 70 percent of girls between 15 and 19 years old had undergone FGM/C, a decrease from 81 percent in 2008. According to the same survey, 93 percent of ever-married women between 15 and 49 years old had undergone FGM/C. The survey showed that 54 percent of mothers supported FGM/C, a decrease from 75 percent in 2000. The Ministry of Health and Population prepared the EHIS in partnership with UNFPA, the UN Children's Fund (UNICEF), and other international partners. In June 2015 the government launched its National Strategy for the Abandonment of FGM/C, led by the Population Ministry in partnership with the United Nations and other international partners.

An amendment to the FGM/C law, issued on September 28, designates the practice a felony, as opposed to a misdemeanor as it was previously, and assigns penalties of five to seven years in prison for practitioners who perform the procedure, or 15 years if the practice led to death or "permanent deformity." Those who "accompany" the girl or woman to the FGM/C procedure are subject to one to three years in prison according to the amendment. The law continued to grant exceptions in cases of "medical necessity," which rights groups identified as a problematic loophole that allowed the practice to continue. According to international and local observers, the government did not effectively enforce the FGM/C law and did not make adequate budget allocations to raise awareness. On May 28, 17-year-old Mayar Moussa died after undergoing an illegal FGM/C procedure at a hospital in Suez Governorate, prompting a critical public reaction. The Office of the Prosecutor General issued arrest warrants for seven suspects involved in the case, and in June authorities referred four of the seven to criminal court. On December 20, a Suez criminal court sentenced the doctor who performed the procedure to five years' imprisonment and a fine of LE 50,000 ($2,750) and sentenced three others, including Moussa's mother, to a one-year suspended sentence and a fine of LE 5,000 ($275).

In July authorities arrested the doctor convicted of manslaughter in January 2015 after performing an illegal FGM/C procedure on 13-year-old Sohair el-Batea, who died as a result. He had initially avoided arrest and continued practicing medicine intermittently, despite his conviction and a court order that his clinic be closed. In November authorities announced they would charge the clinic with violating the closure order. The doctor and the girl's father were the first individuals brought to trial since the 2008 law banned FGM/C.

<u>Other Harmful Traditional Practices</u>: The law does not specifically address "honor" crimes, which are treated as any other crime. There were no reliable statistics regarding the incidence of killings and assaults motivated by "honor," but observers stated such killings occurred, particularly in rural areas. On June 16, police arrested one suspect related to an "honor" crime in Minoufia Governorate after a brother killed his sister for allegedly practicing prostitution.

<u>Sexual Harassment</u>: Sexual harassment remained a serious problem. According to a study published in 2013 by the UN Entity for Gender Equality and the Empowerment of Women, known as UN Women, 99 percent of women and girls in the country's sample reported they had experienced some form of sexual harassment. According to the ECGBVS, more than 1.7 million women suffered from sexual harassment on public transportation. NGOs reported the overall

incidence of sexual harassment increased during times of large public gatherings, such as during holidays.

The government prioritized efforts to address sexual harassment. Since 2014 the penal code has defined sexual harassment as a crime, with penalties including fines and sentences of six months to five years in prison. Media and NGOs reported that sexual harassment by police was also a problem, and the potential for further harassment further discouraged women from filing complaints. There were no reported convictions under the antiharassment law, although media reported many arrests. The NCW reported 91 official complaints of sexual harassment during Eid al-Fitr celebrations in July, while some local media reports cited higher numbers. The outcome of these cases was unclear.

In March 2015 a video circulated on social media of five police officers sexually assaulting and beating two women during a security raid in Daqahliya Governorate. The Ministry of Interior announced it would open an investigation, but it had not announced the results of the investigation by year's end.

Reproductive Rights: The law recognizes the basic right of married couples to decide the number, spacing, and timing of their children; manage their reproductive health; and have access to the information and means to do so, free from discrimination, coercion, or violence. Social, cultural, and religious barriers, however, restricted women's rights to make reproductive decisions and to attain the highest standard of reproductive health. Although the government did not restrict citizens' family-planning decisions, men and women did not always have the information and means to make decisions free from discrimination and coercion. The ECGBVS found that 87 percent of ever-married urban women and 85 percent of ever-married rural women used some form of family planning. According to 2015 estimates by UNFPA, 58 percent of women between the ages of 15 and 49 were using a modern method of contraceptives, and 12 percent of women have an unmet need for family planning.

The Ministry of Health and Population distributed contraceptive materials and provided personnel to attend births, postpartum care to mothers and children, and treatment for sexually transmitted diseases at no cost. According to the 2014 Egyptian Demographic Health Survey (EDHS), published in 2015 by the ministry, 90 percent of mothers received at least some antenatal care from a trained provider, and 83 percent of mothers had at least four antenatal visits. A doctor or trained nurse/midwife assisted at the delivery of 92 percent of all births with 87 percent occurring in a health facility. Some NGOs reported government family planning information and services were not adequate to meet the needs of the population, particularly outside urban areas.

<u>Discrimination</u>: The constitution provides for equal rights for male and female citizens. Women did not effectively enjoy the same legal rights and opportunities as men, and discrimination continued to be widespread. Aspects of the law and traditional practices continued to disadvantage women in family, social, and economic life.

Women continued to face widespread societal discrimination, threats to their physical security, and workplace bias in favor of men that hindered their social and economic advancement. The NCW, members of which the government appointed, led efforts to combat discrimination.

In August, Safaa Hegazy, the director of state-run Egyptian radio and television, barred eight anchorwomen from appearing on the air for a month, saying they were overweight. Hegazy reportedly ordered the women to go on a diet during their suspensions and that unspecified action be taken against them if they were unsuccessful.

Laws affecting marriage and personal status generally corresponded to an individual's religious group. For example, a female Muslim citizen cannot legally marry a non-Muslim man. If she were to do so unofficially, she would face significant societal harassment. Under the government's interpretation of Islamic law, any children from such a marriage could be placed in the custody of a male Muslim guardian. "Khula" divorce allows a Muslim woman to obtain a divorce without her husband's consent, provided she forgoes all her financial rights, including alimony, dowry, and other benefits. The Coptic Orthodox Church permits divorce only in rare circumstances, such as adultery or conversion of one spouse to another religious group. Other Christian churches permitted divorce.

A Muslim female heir receives half the amount of a male heir's inheritance, and Christian widows of Muslims have no inheritance rights. A sole Muslim female heir receives half her parents' estate, and the balance goes to the siblings of the parents or the children of the siblings if the siblings are deceased. A sole male heir, who is expected to provide for relatives, inherits his parents' entire estate.

A woman's testimony is equal to that of a man in courts dealing with all matters except for personal status, such as marriage and divorce. In marriage and divorce cases, a woman's testimony must be judged credible to be admissible. Usually the woman accomplishes this credibility by conveying her testimony through an adult male relative or representative. The law assumes a man's testimony is credible unless proven otherwise.

The law makes it difficult for women to access formal credit. While the law allows women to own property, social and religious barriers strongly discouraged women's ownership of land, a primary source of collateral in the banking system. The threat of criminal bankruptcy and fear of prison conditions contributed to extremely low rates of women accessing commercial credit.

Women faced extensive discrimination in the labor force. Labor laws provide for equal rates of pay for equal work for men and women in the public but not the private sector. In 2014 the World Economic Forum found that women received 78 percent of the income of their male counterparts--not of men in general. Educated women had employment opportunities, but social pressure against women pursuing a career was strong. Women's rights advocates claimed religious influence as well as traditional and cultural attitudes and practices inhibited further gains. Large sectors of the economy controlled by the military excluded women from high-level positions, since women do not serve in the military except in limited specific capacities, and thus did not have access to these jobs. According to the UN Development Program, women represented 23 percent of the labor force. According to the governmental CAPMAS, the female unemployment rate was more than 24 percent, compared with 9.8 percent for men. The Ministry of Social Solidarity operated more than 150 family counseling bureaus nationwide to provide legal and medical services to unemployed women who were unmarried or did not reside with family.

Children

Birth Registration: Children derive citizenship through the citizenship of their parents. The mother or the father transmits citizenship and nationality. The government attempted to register all births soon after birth but some citizens in remote and tribal areas, such as the Sinai Peninsula, resisted registration or could not document their citizenship, thus rendering it difficult to register births. The government cooperated with NGOs in addressing this problem. In some cases failure to register resulted in denial of public services, particularly in urban areas where most services required presentation of a national identification card.

Education: Education is compulsory, free, and universal until the ninth grade. The law provides this benefit to stateless persons and refugees. Some public schools enrolled Syrian refugees, but they largely excluded other nationalities. Other refugee children attended private and community-based schools, if they had the resources or assistance, or were home schooled.

Child Abuse: The constitution defines a child as anyone under the age of 18. It stipulates the government shall protect children from all forms of violence, abuse, mistreatment, and commercial and sexual exploitation. There were widespread reports of child abuse, according to local and international rights groups. According to a local rights group, hundreds of cases were recorded each month, and many cases went unreported. According to UNICEF, at least 80 percent of children between 13 and 17 years old were exposed to some form of violence (physical, emotional, or sexual). No effective government institutions were dedicated to addressing child abuse, although several civil society organizations assisted runaway and abandoned children.

In April a security guard at a private school in Nasr City allegedly raped a three-year-old boy. Family members of the victim claimed that authorities failed to arrest the security guard despite other students identifying him as the attacker and claimed that the forensic report could take up to four months, rather than the 15 days that media reports claimed was average. The Egyptian Coalition for Children's Rights claimed this case highlighted the lack of enforcement of child protection laws.

Rights organizations reported children faced mistreatment in detention, including torture, sharing cells with adults, denial of their right to counsel, and authorities' failure to notify their families. For example, HRW reported that security forces allegedly tortured a group of 20 individuals, eight of them children, in February after arrests in Alexandria. According to HRW, relatives and lawyers said authorities refused to acknowledge holding them or to tell their families their whereabouts for more than a week and tortured them to obtain confessions to crimes or provide the names of other suspects.

In December 2015 AI reported that security forces detained 14-year-old Mazen Mohamed Abdallah in September 2015 and initially held him for seven days without contacting his family. Authorities later charged Abdallah with belonging to a banned group, protesting without authorization, and printing flyers inciting protests. AI reported that authorities tortured Abdallah, including by repeatedly raping him with a wooden stick and subjecting him to electric shocks, while in custody in adult detention facilities in the First Nasr City and the Second Nasr

City. The Interior Ministry denied these claims. On January 31, authorities released Abdallah pending investigation.

Early and Forced Marriage: The legal age of marriage is 18. According to the ECGBVS, 27 percent of girls married before age 18. Among ever-married women between the ages of 18 to 64, 11 percent reported that their consent to marry was never sought. A few women reported that their consent had been sought; they had refused, but the marriage had taken place anyway. As many as 15 percent of all marriages in the country were child marriages (of an unspecified age), according to remarks made by the minister of population to media in August 2015. Media reported some child marriages were temporary marriages intended to mask child prostitution. Families sometimes forced adolescent girls to marry wealthy foreign men in what were known locally as "tourism" or "summer" marriages for the purpose of sexual exploitation, prostitution, or forced labor. According to the law, a foreign man who wants to marry an Egyptian woman more than 25 years younger than he is must pay a fine of LE 50,000 ($2,750). Women's rights organizations argued that allowing foreign men to pay a fine to marry much younger women represented a form of trafficking and encouraged child marriage. They called on the government to eliminate the system altogether. The Antitrafficking Unit at the National Council for Childhood and Motherhood (NCCM), a governmental body, is responsible for raising awareness of the problem.

Female Genital Mutilation/Cutting: See information provided in women's section above.

Sexual Exploitation of Children: The law provides for sentences of not less than five years in prison and fines of up to LE 200,000 ($11,000) for commercial sexual exploitation of children and child pornography. The government did not adequately enforce the law. The minimum age for consensual sex is 18. NGOs and local media reported sex tourism and the number of street children in Cairo and other metropolitan areas (where criminals sometimes sexually exploited children) remained high due to economic hardship. Temporary marriages were also sometimes used to mask sexual exploitation of children and child prostitution.

Displaced Children: Experts who worked with street children struggled to define exactly to whom the term "displaced children" applied, and consequently estimates of the number of children on the streets varied. The Ministry of Social Solidarity estimated the number of street children to be 20,000, while civil society organizations estimated the number to be in the millions. Many were victims of violence and sexual abuse, including forced prostitution. The ministry offered shelters to street children, but many chose not to use them because they closed at night, forcing the children onto the streets. Religious institutions and NGOs provided services for street children, including meals, clothing, and literacy classes. The Ministry of Health and Population offered mobile health clinics staffed by nurses and social workers.

International Child Abductions: The country is not a party to the 1980 Hague Convention on the Civil Aspects of International Child Abduction. See the Department of State's *Annual Report on International Parental Child Abduction* at travel.state.gov/content/childabduction/en/legal/compliance.html.

Anti-Semitism

The country's Jewish community is tiny and dwindling. Criticism of Israel frequently reached the level of blatant anti-Semitism in public discourse. State-owned and private media used anti-Semitic rhetoric, including by academics, cultural figures, and clerics, with cartoons demonizing Jews. There were multiple reports of imams using anti-Semitic rhetoric in their sermons. Societal anti-Semitism was widespread.

In March Members of Parliament (MPs) used MP Tawfik Okasha's meeting with the Israeli ambassador to vote to strip Okasha of his membership. MP Kamal Ahmed struck Okasha in the head with a shoe on the floor of parliament--an act that he said was a "message to Netanyahu and all Zionists."

In May and June, the government-owned newspaper *al-Ahram* published a series of anti-Semitic articles, accusing Jews of "plotting to enslave the world," "claiming that their religion is the only religion," "inventing atheism," "leading countries to religious and political extremism," and staging an "economic takeover of the world." Most of these allegations of "evil" referenced the long-debunked *Protocols of the Elders of Zion.*

In July professor and political activist Mamdouh Hamza posted a series of tweets in which he expressed his opposition to a rumored proposed law to sell Egyptian citizenship. Hamza said he feared Jews who had been forced out of the country in the 1950s and 1960s might return to "overturn Egyptian laws" and "confiscate" land. Media amplified Hamza's statements.

For the sixth consecutive year, authorities cancelled the Abu Hassira celebrations scheduled for January, preventing an annual Jewish pilgrimage, which in previous years had included many Israelis, to the shrine of 19th-century scholar Rabbi Yaakov Abu Hassira. The cancellation followed a 2014 administrative court decision to ban the festival permanently, stating the festival was a "violation of public order and morals" and "incompatible with the solemnity and purity of religious sites."

An appeal continued in the 2014 case of 37 Islamists sentenced to death and 492 others to life imprisonment whom a Minya criminal court described as "demons" who followed Jewish scripture. The court also described the men as "enemies of the nation" who used mosques to promote the teachings of "their holy book, the Talmud." The court had sentenced them for involvement in acts of violence, breaking into and burning a police station, burning police vehicles, stealing weapons, killing one police officer, and attempting to kill another in Minya in 2013. Authorities scheduled the next hearing for January 4, 2017. As of September, 183 of the defendants were in custody pending appeal.

Trafficking in Persons

See the Department of State's *Trafficking in Persons Report* at www.state.gov/j/tip/rls/tiprpt/.

Persons with Disabilities

The constitution states all citizens "are equal in rights, freedoms, and general duties without discrimination based on…disability" among other attributes, but it does not explicitly "prohibit" discrimination.

Although the constitution states persons with disabilities are equal without discrimination before the law, at year's end no laws prohibited discrimination against persons with disabilities in education, air travel and other transportation, the judicial system, access to health care, or the provision of other state services. Nor did laws mandate access to buildings or transportation.

The law provides for persons with disabilities to gain access to vocational training and employment but does not outlaw discrimination altogether. Government policy for employing persons with disabilities is based on a quota (5 percent of workers with disabilities) for companies with more than 50 employees. According to most sources, authorities did not enforce this quota, and companies often had persons with disabilities on their payroll to meet the quota without actually employing them. Widespread discrimination continued against persons with disabilities, particularly persons with mental disabilities, resulting in a lack of acceptance into mainstream society. Government-operated treatment centers for persons with disabilities, especially children, were of poor quality.

The Ministries of Education and Social Solidarity share responsibility for protecting the rights of persons with disabilities. Persons with disabilities rode government-owned mass transit buses without charge, but the buses were not wheelchair-accessible, and access required assistance from others. Persons with disabilities received special subsidies to purchase household products, wheelchairs, and prosthetic devices. Persons with disabilities also received expeditious approval for the installation of new telephone lines and received reductions on customs duties for specially equipped private vehicles.

National/Racial/Ethnic Minorities

The law prohibits discrimination on any grounds. Nevertheless, dark-skinned Egyptians and sub-Saharan Africans faced discrimination and harassment. In particular Nubians from Upper Egypt experienced discrimination because of their skin color or because the public perceived them to be sub-Saharan African migrants or refugees.

According to the constitution, the state should make efforts to return Nubians to their original territories and develop such territories within 10 years of the constitution's 2014 ratification.

In August, President Sisi issued a decree assigning 922 feddans (957 acres) of state-owned land to a new agricultural development project. Nubian rights organizations claimed this would deprive the Nubian community of access to ancestral homelands. In protest of this action, hundreds of Nubians formed a convoy to attempt to access a historical Nubian village incorporated into the state project. On November 19, when security forces blocked the convoy on a highway between the city of Aswan and Abu Simbel, the Nubians began a protest. Related clashes subsequently erupted in Aswan between security forces and protesters, with security forces reportedly firing rubber bullets and live rounds at protesters after they blocked roads and burned tires. Security forces surrounded the protesters' encampment and prevented them from receiving food and water. Senior government officials including the prime minister and members of parliament attempted to negotiate an end to the protests, and the prime minister reportedly promised that Nubians would have priority rights to some of the land in the development project. On November 23, protesters dispersed and begin seeking a resolution with the government through negotiations, according to a Nubian rights lawyer's comments to the press.

Acts of Violence, Discrimination, and Other Abuses Based on Sexual Orientation and Gender Identity

While the law does not explicitly criminalize consensual same-sex sexual activity, it allows police to arrest lesbian, gay, bisexual, transgender, and intersex (LGBTI) persons on charges such as "debauchery," "prostitution," and "violating the teachings of religion" and provides for prison sentences of up to 10 years. According to a local rights group, there were at least 250 reports of such arrests since 2013. Authorities did not use antidiscrimination laws to protect LGBTI individuals. Gay men, lesbians, and transgender persons faced significant social stigma and discrimination, impeding their ability to organize or publicly advocate on behalf of LGBTI persons. Information was not available on official or private discrimination in employment, occupation, housing, statelessness, or access to education or health care based on sexual orientation and gender identity. There were no government efforts to address potential discrimination.

There were few reported incidents of violence against LGBTI individuals, although intimidation and the risk of arrest greatly restricted open reporting and contributed to self-censorship. Rights groups and activists reported harassment by police, including physical assault and forced payment of bribes to provide information about other LGBTI individuals or to avoid arrest. The government has the authority to deport or bar entry to gay foreigners.

There were reports that authorities used social media, dating websites, and cell phone apps to entrap persons they suspected of being gay or transgender, a tool that LGBTI advocates described as especially effective as LGBTI-friendly public spaces had largely closed over the past two years.

On April 24, an Agouza misdemeanor court convicted 11 men of debauchery, incitement to debauchery, and other charges, sentencing three of the 11 to 12 years in prison, three to nine years, one to six years, and four to three years. A local rights group condemned the verdict as part of an orchestrated police campaign against LGBTI individuals. On May 29, an appeals court acquitted one of the defendants and reduced the others' sentences to one-year's imprisonment.

In January the court acquitted television host Mona Iraqi of defaming the 26 arrested men charged with "practicing debauchery" and "indecent public acts." Police had raided a traditional bathhouse known as a hammam in Cairo in 2014 and arrested them, but a misdemeanor court acquitted all 26 in January 2015. Iraqi had posted photographs of the men being dragged out of the hammam on Facebook and had been convicted of publishing false news in November 2015. Her acquittal came after a Cairo court accepted her appeal.

Authorities continued to subject individuals detained on suspicion of debauchery to forced anal examinations, according to a local rights group.

HIV and AIDS Social Stigma

HIV-positive individuals faced significant social stigma and discrimination in society and the workplace. According to the EDHS, fewer than 1 percent of men and women between the ages of 15 and 49 expressed accepting attitudes towards those with HIV/AIDS. The health-care system provided anonymous counseling and testing for HIV, free adult and pediatric antiretroviral therapy, and support groups. Authorities paid insufficient attention to the specific needs of women and children, particularly in the areas of medical treatment, psychosocial support, and the prevention of mother-to-child transmission.

Other Societal Violence or Discrimination

There were incidents of mob violence and vigilantism, particularly sectarian violence against Coptic Egyptians. On May 20, a mob of approximately 300 armed Muslim residents of Minya's el-Karm village attacked seven Christian households after rumors spread of an affair between a Christian man and Muslim woman, according to media reports. The mob burned several Christian-owned homes and stripped naked an elderly Christian woman whom they paraded through the streets. In comments to media, the president promised to hold perpetrators of the violence accountable and repair damaged property at government expense. The armed forces rebuilt damaged property. On October 6, the prosecutor general referred 25 suspects to trial on charges of illegal assembly, arson, vandalism, and illegal possession of firearms. As of year's end, the date for a hearing had yet to be set.

Section 7. Worker Rights

a. Freedom of Association and the Right to Collective Bargaining

The law provides for the rights of workers to form and join independent unions, to bargain collectively, and to strike, with significant restrictions. The constitution provides for freedom of association, but authorities had not drafted implementing legislation. Older labor laws still on the books contradict this right, and in March the Interior Ministry issued a directive instructing government offices not to accept documents stamped by independent trade unions as legal documents, calling such unions "illegitimate entities."

The law provides for collective bargaining but imposes significant restrictions. For example, the government sets wages and benefits for all public-sector employees. The law does not provide for enterprise-level collective bargaining in the private sector but requires centralized tripartite negotiations with workers represented by a union affiliated with the Egyptian Trade Union Federation (ETUF) and the Ministry of Manpower overseeing and monitoring collective negotiations and agreements.

The constitution provides for the right to "peaceful" strikes. The Unified Labor Law permits peaceful strikes but imposes significant restrictions for strikes to be considered legal, including prior approval by a general trade union affiliated with the ETUF.

The law prohibits antiunion discrimination and provides for the reinstatement of workers fired for union activity. Labor laws do not cover several categories of workers, including agricultural and domestic workers, among other sectors of the informal economy.

Government enforcement of applicable laws was inconsistent. On April 30, HRW reported that no new unions had been able to register since September 2015. The government also occasionally used its powers to arrest striking workers and rarely reversed arbitrary dismissals. The government seldom followed the requirement for tripartite negotiations in collective disputes, and workers negotiated directly with employers, usually after resorting to a strike. When the government became involved, it most often was for dispute resolution rather than for genuine collective bargaining.

On March 20, hundreds of public-sector employees organized a demonstration against the civil service law adopted by presidential decree in July 2015. Workers criticized the law for decreasing benefits, which the government stated was necessary for budgetary reform. Parliament rejected the law in January as part of its review of presidential decrees issued in the absence of a legislative body. On October 3, it approved a revised version, and the government issued the law on November 2. Separately, textile workers ended their strike after receiving a written assurance from the president that they would receive the 10 percent "social allowance" promised under the civil service law, according to media reports.

Unions, which had proliferated in recent years, continued to face pressure to dissolve. On June 26, an administrative court referred a lawsuit calling for the dissolution of independent trade unions to the Supreme Constitutional Court. ETUF affiliates filed the lawsuit.

Two main independent trade union federations, the Egyptian Federation of Independent Trade Unions and the Egyptian Democratic Labor Congress, continued to operate. The National Federation of Egyptian Trade Unions, a coalition of 140 independent trade unions from the public and private sector whose leadership stated it focused on negotiations with the government rather than strikes or protests, had not been reported to have engaged in any activities since its founding in October 2015.

While it was no longer directly controlled by the state, observers still saw the ETUF as subordinate to the state, and authorities repeatedly postponed elections for new leadership. Government-appointed ETUF board members remained in place, despite the May 2015 expiration of former prime minister Mehlab's 2014 decree to extend the government-appointed board. The ETUF received some advantages from the state. In June the government did not include independent trade unions in its official delegation to the International Labor Conference in Geneva; however, several independent trade unions participated in the conference at the invitation of the International Labor Organization.

Authorities arrested or subjected to other legal sanctions several labor organizers, often following the dispersal or end of a labor strike. Authorities arrested 27 shipyard workers in Alexandria after a May 22-23 sit-in to protest delayed bonuses and other work-related grievances. Authorities charged the workers with instigating unlawful strikes and obstructing company operation. They were being tried by a military court on the grounds that the shipyard, a former state-owned enterprise, remains under Ministry of Defense administration. In November authorities ordered the workers released on bail after they resigned from the shipyard. The next hearing was scheduled for January 24, 2017.

Workers sometimes staged sit-ins on government and private property, often without obtaining the necessary permits. In June workers from the Nile Cotton Ginning Company staged a sit-in in front of parliament to protest delayed enforcement of a court order to return the company to state ownership after authorities sold it to a private company.

Police, and the military to a lesser extent, engaged in the forceful dispersal of labor actions in isolated cases.

b. Prohibition of Forced or Compulsory Labor

The constitution states no work may be compulsory except by virtue of a law. Government did not effectively enforce the prohibition. Employers subjected male and female persons (including citizens) from South Asia, Southeast Asia, and Africa to forced labor in domestic service, construction, cleaning, begging, and other sectors. The government worked with NGOs to provide some assistance to victims of human trafficking, including forced labor.

Also see the Department of State's *Trafficking in Persons Report* at www.state.gov/j/tip/rls/tiprpt/.

c. Prohibition of Child Labor and Minimum Age for Employment

The Child Law sets the minimum age for regular employment at age 15 and at 13 for seasonal employment. The constitution defines a child as anyone under the age of 18. A Ministry of Manpower decree bars children under age 18 from 44 specific hazardous occupations, while the Child Law prohibits employment of children under 18 from work that "puts the health, safety, or morals of the child into danger." Provincial governors, with the approval of the minister of education, may authorize seasonal work (often agricultural) for children age 12 or older, provided duties are not hazardous and do not interfere with schooling. The labor code and Child Law limit children's work hours and mandate breaks. The labor code explicitly excludes domestic work, work in family businesses, and work in noncommercial agriculture from minimum age and other restrictions.

Overall, authorities did not enforce child labor laws effectively. The Ministry of Manpower, in coordination with the NCCM and the Ministry of Interior, enforced child labor laws in state-owned enterprises and private-sector establishments through inspections and supervision of factory management. Labor inspectors generally operated without adequate training on child labor issues, although the

Ministry of Manpower continued to offer some child-labor-specific training. The government did not inspect noncommercial farms for child labor, and there were very limited monitoring and enforcement mechanisms for children in domestic service. When authorities prosecuted offenders, the fines imposed were often as low as LE 500 ($28), insufficient to deter violations. The government did not enforce child labor laws in the informal sector.

Data was not available on Ministry of Manpower inspections for the use of child labor. Where child labor was found, the ministry issued warnings fines, or it referred the offending companies to the Office of the Prosecutor General.

Although the government often did not effectively enforce relevant laws, authorities continued to implement a number of social, educational, and poverty reduction programs to reduce children's vulnerability to exploitive labor. The NCCM, working with the Ministries of Education and Social Solidarity, sought to provide working children with social security safeguards and to reduce school dropout rates by providing families with alternative sources of income.

Child labor occurred, although estimates on the number of child laborers varied. According to a 2010 report by CAPMAS, the most recent available, 1.594 million children worked, primarily in the agricultural sector in rural areas but also in domestic work and factories in urban areas, often under hazardous conditions. Children also worked in light industry, the aluminum industry, construction sites, and service businesses such as auto repair. According to government, NGO, and media reports, the number of street children in Cairo continued to increase in the face of deteriorating economic conditions. Such children were at greater risk of sexual exploitation or forced begging. In some cases employers abused or overworked children.

Also see the Department of Labor's *Findings on the Worst Forms of Child Labor* at www.dol.gov/ilab/reports/child-labor/findings/.

d. Discrimination with Respect to Employment and Occupation

The constitution states all citizens "are equal in rights, freedoms, and general duties without discrimination based on religion, belief, gender, origin, race, color, language, disability, social class, political or geographic affiliation, or any other reason." It does not specify age, citizenship, sexual orientation or gender identity, or HIV-positive status or other communicable diseases. The law provides for persons with disabilities to gain access to vocational training and employment but does not completely outlaw discrimination. The government did not effectively enforce prohibitions against such discrimination. Discrimination in employment and occupation occurred with respect to women and persons with disabilities (see section 6). Discrimination against migrant workers occurred (see section 2.d.).

An employee facing discrimination can file a report before the local government labor office. If the employee and the employer are unable to reach an amicable settlement, they take the claim to administrative court, which may order the employer to redress the complaint or to pay damages or legal fees. According to local rights groups, implementation of the law was inadequate. Additionally, the lengthy and expensive litigation process could deter employees from filing claims.

e. Acceptable Conditions of Work

The government introduced a monthly minimum wage of LE 1,200 ($66) for government employees and public-sector workers. According to labor rights organizations, the government implemented the minimum wage for public-sector workers but applied it only to direct government employees and included benefits and bonuses in calculating total salaries. Most government workers already earned income equal to or more than the announced minimum wage. For government employees and public-business-sector workers, the government also set a maximum wage limit at 35 times the minimum wage of LE 42,000 ($2,310) per month. There was no private-sector minimum wage. In July CAPMAS estimated the poverty rate in the country to be 28 percent, an increase from its 2013 estimate of 26 percent. The law does not require equal pay for equal work.

The law stipulates a maximum 48-hour workweek for the public and private sectors and provides for premium pay for overtime and work on rest days and national holidays. The labor law prohibits excessive compulsory overtime. The government sets worker health and safety standards, for example prohibiting employers from maintaining hazardous working conditions. The law excludes agricultural, fisheries, and domestic workers from regulations concerning wages, hours, and working conditions.

The Ministry of Manpower is responsible for enforcement of labor laws and standards for working conditions. Due in part to insufficient resources, labor law enforcement and inspections were inadequate. The ministry did not attempt to apply labor standards to the informal sector. Penalties, especially as they were often unenforced, did not appear sufficient to deter violations. By law workers are allowed to remove themselves from situations that endanger health or safety without jeopardy to employment, although authorities did not reliably enforce this right.

The government provided services, such as free health care, to all citizens, but the quality of services was often poor. Other benefits, such as social insurance, were available only to employees in the formal sector.

Many persons throughout the country faced poor working conditions, especially in the informal economy, which employed up to 40 percent of workers, according to some estimates. Domestic workers, agricultural workers, workers in rock quarries, and other parts of the informal sector were most likely to be subjected to hazardous or exploitive conditions. There were reports of employer abuse of citizen and undocumented foreign workers, especially domestic workers. Little information was available on workplace fatalities and accidents.